"Natalie Kertes Weaver has do[ne] . . . [the]ology courses a great service w[ith this] stantive text. Drawing on year[s . . .] theology understandable to a diverse student body. All students, from the super-devout to the religiously indifferent, from cradle Christians to non-Christians, will come to a critical, appreciative, and historically grounded understanding of Christian beliefs and practices. A fantastic text for the contemporary college classroom."

—Mark J. Allman, Merrimack College, and author of *Who Would Jesus Kill? War, Peace, and the Christian Tradition* (Saint Mary's Press, 2008)

"Imagine an introductory college text on religious studies in Christianity that is amazingly readable both for Christians of all denominations and for those who simply want to know more about Christianity but do not want to be 'talked down to.' From the outset, the author of this brilliant little book (just 200 pages) demonstrates herself to be an experienced teacher of students from a range of religious and not-so-religious backgrounds. Natalie Weaver has listened carefully to her students and has struggled along with them to understand what Christianity is all about.

"Enhancing each chapter are down-to-earth examples from everyday life, as well as handy summary charts, maps, and lists of significant events, names, and dates. Each chapter concludes with a list of key terms and current resources for further study.

"This brilliant synthesis provides an important, accurate, and compact review of Christianity—its foundations, history, doctrinal expressions, diversity, prayer, and social outreach, along with its relationship to non-Christian religions and to the world of science and politics. As a professor of graduate students in theology, I will not hesitate to direct my students to this text.

"Natalie Weaver has done all of us who struggle to know and to teach the faith and practice of Christianity a remarkable service. Her book is balanced and learned, while at the same time, providing a timely and eminently accessible analysis so needed in an increasingly global context."

—Conrad T. Gromada, professor of religious studies
Ursuline College

Author Acknowledgments

Teaching and writing about Christian theology is a magnificent challenge and opportunity. I am profoundly grateful to have many and varied conversation partners who help to advance my own understanding of this faith tradition. I am particularly thankful for the authors referred to in the resource sections of this book, whose excellence and scholarship have so contributed to my own thinking and teaching. Their models and insights have been invaluable in the development of this book. Even more, my personal experience as a Catholic Christian, educator, and writer is bolstered and enhanced by the rich dialogue I am privileged to share with the following people:

- my Christian theology students at Ursuline College
- Sr. Dorothy Ann Blatnica, PhD
- Conrad Gromada, PhD, and Annette Gromada
- George Matejka, PhD
- Joann Piotrkowski
- the theology faculty, alumni, and alumnae of Loyola University–Chicago
- the skillful editors and book reviewers who contributed to this text
- my family

Publisher Acknowledgments

Thank you to the following individuals who reviewed this work in progress.

Patrick Flanagan, *St. John's University, Queens, New York*

Matthew A. Shadle, *Loras College, Dubuque, Iowa*

Christian
Thought
and A Primer
Practice

Natalie Kertes Weaver

Created by the publishing team of Anselm Academic.

Printed in the United States of America

7037

ISBN 978-1-59982-073-6

dedication

For Bertha and Patricia,
who have taught Christianity foremost by their example.

Contents

Author's Introduction to Teachers and Students

Thank you for choosing *Christian Thought and Practice: A Primer* for your introduction to Christian theology. I would like to share a few words about why I wrote this book and how I think it can serve the college classroom and reader.

As a teacher, I have encountered thousands of students undertaking the study of Christian thought. I have used many different books, some of which are excellent and are referenced in this book as suggested supplemental reading. With so many good resources out there, you might ask, Why do we need another introduction to Christian thought? My answer derives from my teaching experience.

Today's classrooms are populated with a diverse student body. In my own classes, I find students of all ages, ethnicities, abilities, and aptitudes, as well as a range of religious backgrounds and beliefs. Although I am Roman Catholic and teach at a Catholic institution, my students include Catholic and Protestant Christians, as well as Muslims, Buddhists, Hindus, and adherents of other non-Christian religions. I also frequently encounter students with little or no religious background, as well as students who participate in a religious tradition but have had little opportunity to study their religion formally or academically.

With so much diversity in the classroom, teachers and students are tasked with multiple challenges. Teachers need to facilitate inclusive discussions and choose proper materials that avoid assumptions about what students might think or how they might have been previously taught. Teachers need to attempt to level the classroom through the cultivation of a working vocabulary of terms and ideas, so students of all backgrounds can proceed together in their work and conversation as a class. Teachers must ultimately speak to the comprehension and interest levels of their students, knowing that many will not choose professional specializations in Christian theology and religious studies.

In teaching Christian theology, I have struggled to find materials that speak to my diverse students at an introductory intensity with sufficient breadth. Often books that claim to be introductions simply exceed in scope or depth the register of nonspecialist readers. This book, by contrast, was developed as a genuine introduction for all readers interested in Christian thought, whether Christian or non-Christian. It presupposes no theological background, so it is appropriate even for those who have had no prior study of Christian thought or religion. Although this book presents a thorough and broad architecture of Christian thought and practice, it does not inundate the reader with references, historical case studies, or tangential discussions. Moreover, the book endeavors to be ecumenical in tone and friendly to a broad range of Christian communions as well as other, non-Christian groups.

You will find in this book an orderly discussion of topics, beginning in chapter 1 with an introduction to the term *theology* and a survey of ideas that will surface in any theological investigation. Building on the first chapter, chapter 2 then explores the classical foundations of Christian theology, equipping readers with basic information about Christian uses of the Bible, tradition, reason, and experience. Because these foundations of Christian theology are always encountered contextually, chapter 3 turns to a discussion of key periods in Christian history. Following an established sensitivity to historical context, chapter 4 discusses mainline Christian doctrines. Recognizing that doctrine may vary among Christians of different creeds, chapter 5 explores the history, variety, and differences among major Christian worship communities. Chapters 6, 7, and 8 deal topically with Christian worship and practice, Christian relationships with non-Christian religions, and Christian relationships with secular society. These chapters aim at understanding Christian belief and practice in the world at varying levels of interaction with Christians, other religions, and the polis, or civil society at large. The chapters may be read sequentially, individually, or whatever order best complements your needs. Each chapter concludes with discussion questions, terms for review, and references for additional reading and research.

I hope you will find this book useful in a number of ways. For example, this book may be used as the following:

- the principal textbook for a course on Christian thought. In a traditional 15-week course, students will benefit from reading a chapter from this text every other week, interspersed by reading primary source materials and exemplars for each of the chapter's themes.
- one among several principal textbooks to provide content on Christian thought in a comparative religions course
- a leveling tool, a refresher, or a reference guide in intermediate or advanced theology courses, where knowledge of basic Christian terms, beliefs, practices, varieties, and historical periods are presupposed
- a complement to any advanced study of Christian history, the Bible, ethics, ecclesiology, philosophy, and so on

The study of Christian thought and practice is as important today as ever. Christian thought dialogues with questions of religious pluralism, religious conflict, politics, public policy, medical ethics, legal practice, social sciences, natural history, physics, astronomy, and more. Christian thought has been an indelible contributor to the shape of Western culture for the past two millennia, and it underlies many broadly held assumptions and norms. Christianity continues to inform the faith of more than two billion people worldwide. Readers will find a solid foundational understanding of Christian thought and practice beneficial for any line of work and any discipline of study.

1

First Things First: Beginning Christian Theology

WHAT TO EXPECT

This chapter introduces theology by discussing the following key areas:

- a functional understanding of Christian theology
- aspects of Christian theology
- types of theology
- the audience for theology

A Functional Understanding of Christian Theology

Christian theology has been defined in many ways throughout Christianity's roughly two-thousand-year history. A simple definition might be "the systematic study of Christian beliefs." Other definitions might begin with the word's Greek origin: *theo-logia* means "God-talk," so theology may be thought of as "talk about God." One example of such God-talk is the following biblical description of how and why one ought to relate to God: "The fear of the Lord is the beginning of knowledge" (Proverbs 1:7). Saint Anselm in the eleventh century classically defined theology as *"fides quaerens intellectum,"* usually translated as "faith seeking understanding."

Although defining theology is important, it is equally critical to understand the function of theology, to comprehend what theology does as a way to grasp what theology is. An analogy is helpful. A student in my class reported that she had had a bad car accident. Her car was destroyed, as was a telephone pole. Thankfully, she walked away from the accident with only a bloody nose. In class she said, "I am not a very religious person, but I could have died in that accident. The fact that I survived uninjured made me think there is a God. I have been much more religious ever since." This student was theologizing about her accident as she grappled with the meaning it held for her life. She reevaluated her priorities in light of the belief that God had a purpose for her.

Many of us have had similar moments when something dramatic happened that subsequently reshaped our sense of meaning and purpose. Not only do individuals respond to such experiences in this way, but so do groups. When whole communities of people have shared experiences of great import that define them, they sometimes interpret a divine hand at work in their lives. One sees this phenomenon in the literature that Christians hold sacred, namely the Bible (also called sacred scripture; the terms are used interchangeably in this text). For example, the book of Exodus in the Bible details the Israelites' process of becoming free from slavery in Egypt. Exodus opens with a discussion of how the Israelites had become slaves to the Egyptian pharaoh sometime in the mid-thirteenth century BCE. The Israelite slaves were roughly treated, and because they had no army or resources, it seemed unlikely their situation would improve. The story goes on to tell of the rise of the prophet Moses, a man appointed by God to lead the Israelite people to freedom. Moses foretells a series of unprecedented natural events (see Exodus chapters 7–11) that eventually persuade the pharaoh to release the Israelites. As the Israelites celebrate their freedom, they determine that God alone could make such wondrous things happen. The events constituted the central story around which the Israelites formed their identity as God's chosen people.

Stories about a people's defining experiences are powerful; witness, for example, the continuing effect of stories of the American Revolution and the civil rights movement for American children today. When such stories have a theological meaning, they often become the core of religion, underlying a religion's sacred rituals, books, calendars, holidays, and prayers. For Christians, shared stories of the life and work of Jesus of Nazareth—a first-century Galilean Jew executed under the rule of the Roman governor Pontius

Pilate—became the core of their religious beliefs. These stories, first shared orally, later became the subject of the New Testament of the Bible and the glue that held together an array of culturally, religiously, linguistically, and ethnically diverse people of the first-century Roman Empire.

It is helpful to consider that at the beginning of the Christian era, there were no Christian church buildings or administrative offices, there was not yet a Bible, and there was no formal system of beliefs about who Jesus was or why his life was so important. All people had at the time of Jesus was an experience that transformed their notion of life's purpose and meaning, coupled with faith that Jesus was responsible for that transformation.

Theologians in the beginning centuries of Christian history (often called the patristic era) interpreted this experience of transformation and articulated its meaning. The first function of Christian theology was to develop clear statements of faith, called creeds (derived from the Latin word *credo*, meaning "I believe"), and to begin to pronounce basic Christian doctrine. These early theologians had to look to the foundations, which were the developing books of the Bible, the experiences of the community, their own reasoning and logic, and the emerging tradition. As they sorted through these materials, they developed in councils (or church meetings) creeds that stated what Christians actually believed. Over time the work of Christian theologians in the first and second centuries became increasingly part of the tradition of faith, eventually becoming part of the material that later generations would consider foundations to be interpreted and evaluated in light of their own contemporary experience.

Then, as now, theology is always situated in a particular historical and geographical context. Different questions and challenges engage the community of believers in every era. As a result, theologians are continually challenged to make sense of the faith anew. Influential twentieth-century theologians have thus suggested that theology is best understood by its function as a mediator or interpreter between tradition and culture. Theology serves as the translator and interpreter of the sources of the tradition (such as the Bible or works of earlier theologians) for the broader public, ensuring that the faith is accountable and meaningful to people's present-day experience. By way of example, theologians today must address a range of bioethical issues related to new reproductive technologies that did not exist even twenty years ago. As another example, theologians who investigate "church" as an area of study are tasked with considering whether, how, or to what degree online forums may legitimately constitute church communities.

Aspects of Christian Theology

If the function of theology is to interpret or mediate between the tradition and its present-day context, then one must ask what aspects of the tradition theology interprets. Theology attempts to interpret, study, and integrate systematically such areas of Christian belief as foundations, the Bible, philosophy, morality and ethics, doctrine, church teaching, and application to human experience.

Foundations in this context refers to the basic sources that theology uses to ground and support Christian belief. Foundational theological questions include, What can we know about God? and, How are people able to experience God communicating with them? Another foundational question might be, Can God be found in nature? Theology requires dependable sources or foundations in order to begin answering even the most basic religious questions. In the Christian belief system, the Bible, tradition, reason, and experience are the principle foundations of theological inquiry.

Study of the Bible refers to the study of the writings that Christians believe are holy and inspired by God. Most Christians believe that God reveals Godself throughout the books of the Bible. The idea that God is revealed in the Bible is called revelation. Although most Christians believe in revelation, the meaning of the term *revelation* can vary. Possible meanings include the literal word of God, the unfolding of God's actions in history, personal insight or inspiration, and the record of God's direct self-disclosure. Those who study the Bible attempt to understand many things about it, including what the text actually says, how to understand the claim that it is God's revelation, how Christians should best interpret the Bible, and how it should direct the lives of Christians today.

Philosophy refers to the ancient discipline that investigates epistemology (the study of the nature of knowledge), metaphysics (the study of the nature of the world), and morality (how people should act). Philosophy and theology are closely related, so much so that philosophy has been called the "handmaid of theology." Individually, theology and philosophy are interested in the pursuit of ultimate truth, but they use different foundations. Where philosophy relies on human reason alone, theology uses the Bible and Christian doctrine, as well as human reason. Throughout Christian history, Christians have been in dialogue with the major philosophies of the day.

Morality and ethics are dimensions of philosophy that overlap with theology. Both philosophy and theology are interested in understanding not only what is right and wrong (ethics) but also how people should act based on what they believe to be right (morality). Christian moral theology investigates the question of right action with respect to its faith-based commitments. For example, a Christian moral theologian might consider a question of medical ethics by beginning with the belief that God creates all human beings with inalienable dignity and purpose. One might bring many considerations to the question of medical ethics, but a Christian medical ethics will be guided by the moral principle of dignity of life. The study of both morality and ethics straddles many facets of society. Christian investigation of ethical questions and moral living will be guided by a faith-based understanding of the meaning, purpose, and value of human life.

Doctrine refers to the specific Christian beliefs or teachings that theologians study and sometimes help to develop. Examples of Christian doctrine include that Jesus is God incarnated (from a Latin term that literally means "enfleshed") in human life, that God is three in one, and that Jesus was born of the Virgin Mary. Many key beliefs of Christian faith are complex. For example, Christians typically proclaim that Jesus' death saves humanity from sin. This statement raises many questions. Why did Jesus die? Was it necessary, or did it just happen? What is sin? Why do human beings need to be saved from sin, and what does salvation look like? What is the scope of salvation: is it for everyone, or just Christians, or just very good Christians?

Theologians in every age study doctrine to evaluate and make sense of the basic claims Christians hold as truths of their faith.

Church teaching in the form of documents and the written resources of the tradition (beyond the Bible itself) are one way that doctrines and teachings are preserved and passed down from one generation to the next. Examples of such written documents include letters and treatises by notable Christian thinkers and leaders, papers and records of church councils and synods throughout the ages, statements of the faith called *creeds*, and biblical commentaries. Theologians study written documents to see how statements of Christian faith have developed over time. Though a doctrine itself may not change, the way it is communicated or described in church documents may change from time to time based on cultural contexts. For example, modern thought has entertained a number of questions about the origins of the natural world since the theory of evolution was first proposed in the nineteenth century. While Christians had always maintained that God creates the world, it was unnecessary to deal with the theory of evolution before its introduction. Faith that God creates the world has not changed, but the way many Christians talk about creation today now acknowledges evolutionary theory.

Applications of Christian faith to human experience is an important component of Christian theology. To grasp this idea, it is useful to recognize that all knowledge is located in human "knowers." It is people who think about mathematics, who perform scientific experiments, who theorize about the purpose of literature, and so on. Even the most abstract ideas need human beings to think them. Take the various scientific disciplines, for example. Through scientific studies, people attempt to know and understand the world to the best of humanity's ability at any point in time. Scientists share this task across disciplines and perspectives. An urban planner and an ecologist, for example, look at the problem of pollution differently, but both are evaluating the same phenomenon. All disciplines of science use special methods, principles, and instruments.

Theology is no different in this way from science and other types of human knowing. It, too, derives from human ability and experience. If God reveals, it is human beings who receive that revelation within the context of ordinary human life, contingent on personal and social contexts. Theologians are interested in the same world that scientists study. Theologians might also be interested in the problem of pollution in urban settings, but their approach to it would be informed by assumptions specific to the theological discipline. So theologians might see the problem of pollution as a justice issue, as a violation of God's creation, or as an issue of human dignity. In a sense, theology might be thought of as the work of ordinary people reflecting on ordinary experiences made extraordinary by the insights the experiences reveal about human beings, their world, and the meaning and purpose of life.

A NOTE ON THEOLOGICAL METHOD

All academic disciplines use methods of inquiry, and theology is no different. Paying attention to the method one uses when doing theology is key to doing theology well. Thinking about method reminds theologians that they are making choices about what to study, what to attend to, and what temporarily to set aside. An awareness of method also reminds theologians that they are not value-neutral observers making objective interpretations about the material they are studying. People in twenty-first-century America, for example, largely assume that women and men should be treated equally under the law and in most or all areas of society. This assumption affects how theologians today view women in the Bible or in historical theology. By contrast, people in fifteenth-century Europe did not assume gender equality, so their readings of the Bible or doctrine would have been different. Being aware of method means understanding that one's approach to theology is itself an ethical judgment about oneself as an interpreter and about what one thinks is necessary and important about theology. Theologians may employ many methods, but every method involves a choice (even if unconscious) about how to engage the material being studied.

Types of Theology

Just as there are many aspects of the work theologians do, so also are there many types of theology. In a sense, it is more proper to speak of Christian *theologies* than of a single Christian theology. The type of theology that one does reflects the specific function that theology serves in its role as interpreter and mediator. It will also shape the method one uses for practicing theology and the foundations a theologian prioritizes. Some of the most important theologies people do today include biblical theology, systematic theology, historical theology, pastoral theology, liberation theology, natural theology, and mystical theology.

Biblical theology deals with scholarly study and analysis of the Bible. This fundamental study itself involves many areas of specialization. Some scholars study the Bible at close range, looking at such fine aspects as the condition and reliability of ancient manuscripts, study of biblical languages, study of literary forms used in ancient cultures, the historical context of the Bible, philosophical approaches to biblical translation and interpretation, biblical archaeology, and more. Other scholars study the Bible for its merit as a persuasive or rhetorical book, its doctrinal themes and teachings, its teachings about the nature of the church, and its teachings about Christian moral conduct. The basic assumption of biblical theology is that the Bible must be well understood (and what we cannot understand must be acknowledged) if it is to be a useful foundation for the rest of Christian faith.

Systematic theology is the study of the interconnections among theological doctrines and sources. The aim of systematic theology is twofold: to articulate the inherent reasonability of Christian theology and to present the whole system of teachings in a reasonable and clear way for educational purposes. Systematic theologians debate how best to structure the presentation of ideas. For example, some would begin with the notion of revelation in Scripture, while others would begin with the doctrine of God. In any event, systematic theology aims to assemble the pieces of Christian faith into a coherent whole, as one would fit the pieces of a puzzle together to make a complete picture. Some contemporary theologians prefer the term *constructive theology* to describe the integrative study of doctrines and sources.

Historical theology is the study of how historical eras and contexts affect the development and articulation of beliefs. Because theology is always done within a specific time and place for a specific community of people, theology and its context of origin are indelibly related. In the early Christian era, for example, Christians struggled to negotiate cultural differences between Jewish followers of Jesus and pagan converts to Christianity. Jewish law forbade Jews from eating with non-Jews, which raised questions over whether both groups could celebrate Christian communion (sometimes called the Eucharist, the Last Supper, or the Lord's Supper) together. Although a prominent concern among the first Christians, this particular issue matters little to modern Christians. Modern Christians, however, continue to have questions about who can celebrate communion together. The concern today is not one of pagan or Jew but rather of different Christian groups. Since the time of the Protestant Reformation, Christians have separated themselves into different denominations, many of which will not celebrate the ritual meal together. Theology from both eras will reflect the concerns of the day, as both groups have attempted to understand the meaning and proper form for celebrating the Lord's Supper. Study of historical theology is also central in sorting out how and why some ideas came to be considered orthodox (correct), while others were determined to be heresy (unorthodox, corrupt, or incorrect).

Pastoral theology is concerned with the social application of theological statements. This theology ensures that Christian faith is not limited only to orthodoxy (i.e., thinking right thoughts about God) but also extends to orthopraxy (i.e., doing right things for people). Pastoral theology would note that it is one thing to worry over the proper form and meaning of the Lord's Supper and another to make sure that the people in one's local community actually have supper. It is one thing to theorize about why Christians should have hope in light of the claim that Jesus has saved them. It is another to help a person dying of terminal illness to actually find hope in the face of suffering and death. Pastoral theology strives to bridge the academic and applied dimensions of Christian faith.

Liberation theology refers to numerous twentieth- and twenty-first-century theologies that take a strong interest in the political implications of Christian faith as a force for social liberation. Emerging from the abject poverty of Central and South America in the 1960s, liberation theology pointed out that the Bible reveals a God who is concerned about the plight of the poor. Contemporaneous with Latin American liberation theology was the black theology movement in the United States, which brought out the religious dimension of the civil rights movement. Beginning with these expressions, today's liberation theologies evaluate the condition of all manner of poverty and oppression. These include a wide range of social, political, economic, racial, and gender oppressions. Feminist, Hispanic, African American, womanist, *mujerista* (which blends feminist, Latin American liberation, and cultural theologies), third-world, and LBGTQ (lesbian, bisexual, gay, transgender) theologies are all expressions of liberation theologies seeking justice, inclusion, and voice for their constituencies.

Natural theology studies where God may be found in nature, even without the benefit of special revelation, such as that found in the Bible. Natural theology looks at things like beauty, design, order, and causality in the natural world and evaluates whether and how these aspects suggest a Creator. Modern cosmology and natural theology today engage in exciting dialogue about the origin, destiny, value, and meaning of the natural world.

Mystical theology focuses on the emotional experience of encountering God. This type of theology attempts to put into words experiences that transcend definition. Just as people attempt to describe the experience of falling in love, even as they realize that words cannot describe the experience, so also does mystical theology attempt to describe the conditions and the experience of falling in love with God, being touched by God in prayer and contemplation, or having a direct encounter with God. Mystical theology might thus be thought of as the study of Christian spirituality, prayer, and contemplative practice.

The Audience for Theology

Now that we know something about what theology is and what it does, we might ask, Who is the audience for theology? The highly esteemed Roman Catholic theologian David Tracy has suggested that there are three principal and sometimes overlapping audiences for theology: the church, the academy, and the public.

Church refers to the collective body of Christians (as opposed to church buildings or institutionalized denominations, such as Catholics or Baptists). The church is the primary audience of Christian theology because it is Christians' beliefs that are being considered. Christians' modern experiences raise specific questions about the application of their faith to those experiences. Presumably, Christians are those most invested in understanding Christian thought and belief. For example, non-Christians may want to know what Christian theologians are saying about birth control or new reproductive technologies. It will be Christians themselves, though, who look to theologians for guidance on how to apply Christian beliefs and understandings into their family planning. Like the average Christian layperson (nonclergy), clergy, as well as church administrators, consult theologians on the key questions of the day.

The term *academy* refers to colleges and universities where theology is a discipline of scholarly research and teaching. Since the Middle Ages, theology has been an important part of university curricula. As part of a university, theology departments need to meet the same standards and requirements as other disciplines. These standards and requirements can be established in many ways: through licensure boards, criteria for publishing, national organizations, and so on. Standards and requirements also link disciplines. A sociology student, for example, needs to write papers according to the standards taught in the English department. The key to standards and requirements is that they are shared and public. This is how research, teaching, and publication in any discipline is made accountable and preserves the integrity of its methods and discourse. Like the sociology student mentioned above, students of theology must be intelligently and integratively in dialogue with people in other disciplines. Theologians cannot well advance their discussions of, for example, natural theology if they are ignorant of biology, physics, or chemistry. By being accountable to and in dialogue with other disciplines, theology maintains its status as an important conversation partner in academia.

Public refers to the broad body politic, that is, people in general. Theologians cannot pursue their work with integrity if they ignore basic issues and situations in society. Theologians must acknowledge that Christianity and its ecclesial communions, or denominations, are part of the secular world. Although some Christian groups remain sectarian (or largely detached from the world), theology has a responsibility to understand the world at large and to attempt to hold a dialogue with it as much as possible. Apart from this dialogue, theology would bury its head in the sand, and this would be a failure to perform its basic function as mediator and interpreter between the religious tradition and society. In addition, if theology is not public and open, it risks becoming cultlike and unaccountable, with the added risk of exploiting the people who take direction from it. Being accountable to the public is a safeguard against untenable and detached ideas. It is also the way theology can engage and even persuade the broad public about its constructive and prosocial beliefs, values, and works.

Conclusion

Twentieth-century Brazilian Roman Catholic theologians Leonardo and Clodovis Boff said of theology, "All who believe want to understand something of their faith. As soon as you think about faith, you are already doing theology. So all Christians are in a sense theologians, and become more so the more they think about their faith."[1]

All people who think about their faith and try to understand what it means for their life are doing theology on some level. Professional theologians think, speak, and write about faith all the time. Practitioners and pastoral workers may use theology to help shape

---

[1] Leonardo and Clodovis Boff, *Introducing Liberation Theology* (Maryknoll, NY: Orbis, 1987), 16.

their workplace ethics or their client care. Clergy may use theology to help them write poignant and timely sermons. Stay-at-home moms and dads may use theology to help them get through rough days with noisy kids and piles of laundry.

Although it can be highly academic and refined, theology is ultimately the Christian endeavor to make sense of the beliefs that the faith proclaims. People do theology across all levels of personal interest and professional practice. Theology may be done by highly educated scholars, but it is also the domain of average people attempting to think meaningfully and seriously about what they believe and how those beliefs should shape their lives.

Questions for Discussion and Review

1. How would you describe theology to a child?
2. Give an example of theologizing.
3. What are the poignant moments in life—joyful or tragic—that might prompt a person to think about God?
4. Describe the function of theology as mediator and interpreter and give an example of a current event or situation that could benefit from the mediation of theology.
5. What is the relationship between faith and reason?
6. What is theological method? Is it important? Explain.
7. Give an example of how historical and geographical context can influence theology.
8. Is every religious person a theologian? Explain.
9. Describe and compare two types of theology considered in this chapter.
10. Why is it important for theology to have a public character?

Key Terms

Bible

biblical theology

church

councils

creeds

doctrines

epistemology

function of theology

handmaid of
  theology

heresy

historical theology

liberation theology

metaphysics

natural theology

orthodoxy

orthopraxy

pastoral theology

philosophy

sectarian

systematic theology

theological method

Resources

Boff, Leonardo and Clodovis. *Introducing Liberation Theology.* Mary-knoll, NY: Orbis, 1987.

Bultmann, Rudolph. *What Is Theology?* Minneapolis: Fortress, 2000.

Ford, David. *Theology: A Very Short Introduction.* New York: Oxford University Press, 2000.

Lonergan, Bernard. *Method in Theology.* 2nd ed. Toronto: University of Toronto Press, Scholarly Publishing Division, 1990.

McGrath, Alister E. *Christian Theology: An Introduction.* Oxford, UK: Blackwell, 2011.

Ormerod, Neil. *Introducing Contemporary Theologies: The What and the Who of Theology Today.* Maryknoll, NY: Orbis, 2002.

Tracy, David. *Blessed Rage for Order: The New Pluralism in Theology.* Chicago and London: University of Chicago Press, 1996.

2

Foundations of Christian Theology

WHAT TO EXPECT

This chapter introduces the four principle sources or foundations of Christian theology: Scripture, tradition, reason, and experience. The following key areas of these sources are discussed:

- Scripture (the Bible): Old Testament, New Testament, and Scripture scholarship
- tradition: biblical, extrabiblical, informal
- reason: Christian revelation and reason in dialogue
- experience: hermeneutical circle of praxis and theory

Scripture

Scripture, or the Bible, refers to the forty-six books of the Old Testament (thirty-nine in Hebrew and seven in Greek)[1] and the twenty-seven books of the New Testament that Christians recognize as having divine authority for thought and worship. This collection of seventy-three books comprises what is known as the biblical canon. Although there are other, related books called Apocrypha (a Greek term meaning "hidden writings") or pseudepigrapha ("false writings") that are written by people of the same eras as the authors of the Bible, Christians believe the biblical canon has a special authority and is different in essence from all other written works. This

---

[1] Roman Catholics identify forty-six books as belonging to the Old Testament, while Protestants identify thirty-nine books. These differences will be explored later in this chapter.

authority comes from the Christian belief that the Bible uniquely contains God's revelation.

What is revelation and how is it manifested in the Bible? These questions do not have quick and easy answers, and investigation into the nature of revelation is itself a major aspect of systematic and biblical theology. For the purposes of this discussion, however, revelation may be understood as God's self-disclosure to people revealing what God is like and, further, how people should act in light of the knowledge of God.

We might ask why people need to be told about God. The Christian tradition answers that although God is present in nature and thus naturally accessible on some level by human reason, human beings cannot know the full truth about God apart from God's willing it and intentionally making it so. By way of analogy, consider that people need to tell each other about themselves. We learn only part of the truth about someone by reading his résumé or looking at her artwork. If we want to know someone fully, we need to encounter him personally, and he must disclose something about himself to us. Christian faith holds that this is precisely how God encounters people, and thus how people experience God, and so it has been throughout history.

In the history of Christianity, the Bible emerged as people orally transmitted and eventually wrote down descriptions of revelatory experiences, insights, and encounters that they deemed sufficiently definitive or authoritative to preserve for the good of the present and future community. As these writings became broadly distributed and celebrated, the writings themselves came to be seen as part of the experience of divine revelation (as opposed to merely a record of revelation). Moreover, as these writings were read aloud and shared in the context of Christian worship, the experience of preaching and hearing the writings came to be seen as yet another aspect of divine revelation. Today revelation in the Bible can be thought of as having at least three layers:

- the original revelatory experiences
- the text or written record of revelation experiences
- the oral reading or preaching of the written text

Who had these revelatory experiences, insights, and encounters that became the Bible? They belonged to the early Israelites and to the first followers of Jesus in the emergent Christian movement. These two groups, respectively, composed, edited, and transmitted the books of the Old and New Testaments.

DIVINE INSPIRATION

The issue of divine inspiration is closely related to the discussion of revelation in the Bible. A classic way in which Christians speak about biblical revelation is by saying that the Bible is "the word of God." The phrase *the word of God* and the idea of divine inspiration can both be interpreted in many different ways. The word of God could refer quite literally to God's words, and divine inspiration could refer to the intellectual or mechanical process by which people receive God's words. The word of God could also refer to the mind of God or the wisdom of God. Christians often refer to Jesus himself as the Word of God because they understand him to be the one who is fully God and also fully human, and this in the very constitution of his being, i.e., that he is God Incarnate.

Divine inspiration is not only the word of God. Christians have also used the idea of divine inspiration to explain the internal disposition or awareness within human beings that enables people to read, hear, and understand the word of God in the Bible. Divine inspiration has also been used to explain how people can translate the Bible from one language to another. In a looser sense, divine inspiration may be used to explain the process by which a person creatively yet accurately preaches on the Bible, theologizes about it, or teaches the faith. Many churches, moreover, claim that they are led by the divine inspiration of the Holy Spirit in their actions, teachings, and leadership structures.

The key concept behind the idea of divine inspiration is that when a person or a text or a teaching is believed to originate in God, it has a unique authority over Christians. The roots of the word *inspire* are the prefix *in-* and the verb *spirare* ("to breathe"). Literally, inspiration is a "breathing into." In Christian understanding, something that is inspired is "breathed into" by God.

Old Testament

The Old Testament is a compilation of forty-six books (thirty-nine for Protestants), dating from about 2000 to 100 BCE and written by the biblical Israelites, mostly in Hebrew, with parts in Aramaic and Greek. The Old Testament is identified by several names, including the Hebrew Bible, the First Testament, and the Tanakh. Modern Jews and Christians regard these books as sacred, although both groups identify the collections by different names.

Christians commonly refer to the collection as the Old Testament because it comes before the New Testament. Christians today sometimes prefer the terms *Hebrew Scriptures* or *Hebrew Bible*, respecting that these books belonged first to the Hebrew people and attempting to avoid the possible implication that the Hebrew portion of the Christian Bible is "old" as in the sense of "outdated" or as replaced by the "new." Although the terms *Hebrew Scriptures* and *Hebrew Bible* respect the Hebrew origins of the books, the terms fail to communicate the way that Christians read these books as sequentially preceding the New Testament. As a result, other Christians today prefer the term *First Testament*, to stress continuity with the Second Testament (i.e., the New Testament), while avoiding the implication that the Hebrew texts are outmoded.

People of Jewish faith refer to their sacred literature as the Tanakh, which is an acronym made from the first letters of the Hebrew words *Torah, Nevi'im*, and *Kethuvim*. These words mean "law," "prophets," and "writings," respectively, and each signifies a distinct collection of these Scriptures. Christians organize these books slightly differently, adding a fourth division, history, to the other three. For the most part, the books and translations are the same, but there are a few notable differences.

By the beginning of the Christian era, a Greek translation of the Hebrew Scriptures (known as the Septuagint) was widely circulated. The Greek translation was produced after the Greek armies of Alexander the Great conquered the Israelite people (ca. 333 BCE) and the Greek language became predominant. This Greek collection included seven books (see table, p. 22, Catholic, Protestant Old Testament, and Jewish Tanakh) for which Hebrew translations were nonexistent (either because they were lost near the time of the Greek translation or because the books were composed in Greek). These books are called the *deuterocanon*, meaning "second canon." Though Hebrew rabbis eventually excluded the Greek books from the Jewish canon, Christians preserved them, and they remained part of the Christian Bible until the Protestant Reformation in the sixteenth century. Protestant Reformers eliminated the seven Greek books from their versions of the Old Testament so as to match the Hebrew canon, but Roman Catholic and Orthodox Christians retained them. Despite differences in arrangement and number, today Jews and Christians see the Old Testament/Tanakh as God's revelation.

CATHOLIC, PROTESTANT OLD TESTAMENT, AND JEWISH TANAKH

CATHOLIC OLD TESTAMENT	PROTESTANT OLD TESTAMENT	TANAKH (JEWISH BIBLE)
Pentateuch	Pentateuch	Torah (Law)
Genesis	Genesis	Genesis
Exodus	Exodus	Exodus
Leviticus	Leviticus	Leviticus
Numbers	Numbers	Numbers
Deuteronomy	Deuteronomy	Deuteronomy
Historical Books	Historical Books	Nevi'im (Prophets)
Joshua	Joshua	Joshua
Judges	Judges	Judges
1 & 2 Samuel	1 & 2 Samuel	1 & 2 Samuel
1 & 2 Kings	1 & 2 Kings	1 & 2 Kings
1 & 2 Chronicles	1 & 2 Chronicles	Isaiah
Ezra	Ezra	Jeremiah
Nehemiah	Nehemiah	Ezekiel
Tobit*	Esther	Twelve Minor Prophets
Judith*		Hosea
Esther		Joel
1 Maccabees*		Amos
2 Maccabees*		Obadiah
Wisdom and Poetry	Wisdom and Poetry	Jonah
Job	Job	Micah
Psalms	Psalms	

Continued

Continued Wisdom and Poetry	Wisdom and Poetry	Twelve Minor Prophets
Proverbs Ecclesiastes (also called Qoheleth) Song of Songs (also called Song of Solomon or Canticle of Canticles) Wisdom* Sirach* (also called Ecclesiasticus)	Proverbs Ecclesiastes (also called Qoheleth) Song of Songs (also called Song of Solomon or Canticle of Canticles)	Nahum Habakkuk Zephaniah Haggai Zechariah Malachi
Prophets	**Prophets**	**Kethuvim (Writings)**
Isaiah Jeremiah Lamentations Baruch* Ezekiel Daniel Hosea Joel Amos Obadiah Jonah Micah Nahum Habakkuk Zephaniah Haggai Zechariah Malachi *Seven deutero-canonical books	Isaiah Jeremiah Lamentations Ezekiel Daniel Hosea Joel Amos Obadiah Jonah Micah Nahum Habakkuk Zephaniah Haggai Zechariah Malachi	Psalms Proverbs Job The Scrolls • Song of Songs • Ruth • Lamentations • Ecclesiastes • Esther Daniel Ezra Nehemiah 1 & 2 Chronicles

The major divisions of law, history, prophets, and writings suggest the basic content of these writings. The books of law (which Christians call the Pentateuch, from a Greek word meaning "five books") explain the origin of God's covenant (or binding relationship) with the Israelites and delineate the religious, priestly, and social obligations that the covenant entailed. The books of history present the major events and persons associated with the rise, duration, fall, and restoration of the Kingdom of Israel. The books of the prophets record the words and deeds of Israel's spiritual conscience, whose principal role was to evaluate the religious integrity of the kingdom and its leaders. The books of writings are spiritual reflections on what it means to live a proper life in relationship to God and people.

These books are an important foundation for Christian theology because the Israelite culture and history they record formed the context from which Jesus and the first Christians emerged. Moreover, Jesus and other key figures in the New Testament often refer to the books of the Old Testament. Indeed, the various groups of

TIME LINE OF THE HEBREW BIBLE

2000–1800 BCE	Period of patriarchs and matriarchs (founders of twelve tribes of Israel)
1500–1250	Life in Egypt up through the time of the Exodus
1250–1020	Settlement in Canaan (also called Palestine)
1020–930	United monarchy under kings Saul, David, and Solomon
930–586	Divided monarchy, with Israel (northern kingdom) falling to Assyria in 722 and Judah (southern kingdom) falling to Babylon in 586
586–539	Babylonian Exile (the Israelites forced to live in Babylon) and the destruction of Jerusalem
539–425	Return of Israelites to Palestine and birth of modern Judaism under Ezra and Nehemiah
333–175	Conquest of Palestine by Alexander the Great and Greek occupation
174 BCE–64 CE	Jewish revolt from rulers following the death of Alexander the Great and the establishment of the Jewish Hasmonean Dynasty
63–175 CE	Conquest of Palestine by Roman general Pompey and the onset of Roman occupation

Jewish leaders mentioned in the New Testament make little sense apart from their history, presented in the Hebrew literature. Perhaps most important, the effect that the life of Jesus had on his followers is best understood in light of the tumultuous history to which the Old Testament bears witness.

New Testament

The New Testament is a compilation of twenty-seven books, dating from roughly 50–120 CE and authored in Greek by early Christians. The New Testament is sometimes called either the Second Testament or the Christian Scriptures. These books detail the life of Jesus, the birth of the Christian church, and the beliefs and practices of the first Christian communities. The New Testament books represent four major genres (or types of literature): Gospels, the Acts of the Apostles, Epistles (letters), and apocalyptic literature.

Matthew, Mark, Luke, and John are the four Gospels of the New Testament. Mark, the earliest, was probably written sometime between 66 and 74 CE. Matthew and Luke were likely written between 80 and 90. John is usually dated ca. 100 CE. These four books were anonymously written, but Christian custom attributes them to persons whose names are on the books. The Gospels are the only four books of the Bible that portray the life and teachings of Jesus. Culminating in the story of Jesus' death and Resurrection, the Gospels were written to spread the "good news" (the literal meaning of *gospel*) about Jesus. Even though they do not satisfy the criteria of modern biography, they are the best sources Christians have today for learning about Jesus' life and its effect on his followers.

The book Acts of the Apostles was written by the author of the Gospel of Luke and functions as its sequel. Although the Gospel of Luke describes the life of Jesus, Acts describes the rise of the church after Jesus' ascension into heaven. Appropriately named, the book is an account of the acts of the first Christians, especially Peter and Paul, as they spread their new faith throughout the Roman Empire. Many look at this work as the first church history.

The Epistles are the letters of the New Testament, dating from about 50 CE to the mid-second century. These letters offer teachings on the beliefs and conduct of the emergent Christian communities.

Without benefit of established organizational structures, official doctrines, or leadership models, the first Christians were tasked with developing all three. Through the circulation of letters, the technologically primitive Christian communities (separated by geography, language, and long silences) were able to build consensus on matters of leadership, morals, practices, and core beliefs.

COMMENTARY ON THE NEW TESTAMENT EPISTLES

There are twenty-one Epistles, or letters, in the New Testament. Thirteen of these New Testament letters are attributed to the Apostle Paul, who was instrumental in spreading Christianity through his mission activities in the middle of the first century. A fourteenth letter (the Epistle to the Hebrews) was included in the canon only because Christians came to believe that Paul had authored it, even though there are no such claims in the letter itself. Of the thirteen letters attributed to Paul, most scholars believe seven were actually authored by him (Romans, 1 and 2 Corinthians, Galatians, Philippians, 1 Thessalonians, and Philemon), whereas the other six (Ephesians, Colossians, 2 Thessalonians, 1 and 2 Timothy, and Titus) are understood to be pseudonymous, or falsely ascribed to Paul. The remaining seven of the twenty-one New Testament letters are attributed to important leaders of the early Christian movement, namely Peter (two letters), John (three letters), James (one letter), and Jude (one letter), but scholars debate whether these individuals actually authored the letters that bear their names.

One of the difficult aspects of studying the New Testament letters is that they were written much the same way people write letters today. For example, let's say two friends stay in touch by correspondence, and one of them has a difficult situation going on (a bad romance, loss of a job, and trouble at school, all in one semester). Imagine further that one friend throws out her letters

Continued

Continued

while the other occasionally saves hers. The saved letters eventually are stored in a box in the recipient's basement, until years later when a grown child finds her now-deceased mother's old correspondence. It would be possible to make sense of some of the content of the letters by attempting to recreate their context, but much would be lost because the reader would have only some of what was written, by only one of the two parties writing, about situations that happened long ago, and about which the reader has only a partial understanding.

When studying the New Testament letters, readers encounter similar difficulties. The letters are often situational, dealing with specific questions or circumstances that individuals and churches faced long ago and that the contemporary reader does not fully understand. In addition, some of the original correspondence was lost over time, so only a partial record remains. Further, the true author can't be known for certain, as authors sometimes borrowed a trusted leader's name (such as Paul's) when writing, in order to be more persuasive with readers of the day. Study of the New Testament letters can feel much like a historical scavenger hunt that leads to fascinating, if not definitive, insight into the beliefs, practices, and struggles of the developing Christian church in the first decades after Jesus.

The book of Revelation is the only work in the apocalyptic genre in the New Testament. This final book of the Bible was written by John of Patmos in the late first century CE. The work is part of the "Johannine literature." This collection of books includes the Gospel of John, 1, 2, and 3 John, and Revelation. Although it is likely that a number of authors contributed to this collection, the books bear thematic similarities, indicating they were produced by and for members of an early Christian group, known as the Johannine community. Revelation focuses on the end of the present world and the events that will usher in the world to come. This book simultaneously reveals and hides its messages with the use of ambiguous language and imagery. Although its meaning is not entirely clear, Revelation was likely intended to give hope to Christians who experienced suffering under the persecution of Roman emperors Nero (54–68) and Domitian (81–96).

The books of the New Testament (see table this page, Books and Chronology of the New Testament) provide the story of Jesus'

BOOKS AND CHRONOLOGY OF THE NEW TESTAMENT

BOOKS OF THE NEW TESTAMENT	APPROXIMATE CHRONOLOGY OF THE NEW TESTAMENT
Gospels and Acts	
Matthew	63 BCE Beginning of Roman occupation
Mark	of Palestine
Luke	
John	40 Romans appoint Herod as Jewish king
Acts of the Apostles	
Epistles and Revelation	6–4 BCE Birth of Jesus
Romans	
1 Corinthians	26–36 CE Pontius Pilate made procurator
2 Corinthians	of Judea (lands of Palestine)
Galatians	
Ephesians	27–30 Jesus' ministry, ending in his
Philippians	Crucifixion
Colossians	
1 Thessalonians	
2 Thessalonians	30–50 Early Christian movement and dis-
1 Timothy	semination of oral traditions about Jesus
2 Timothy	
Titus	
Philemon	50–60 Paul composes his letters
Hebrews	
James	66–73 Jewish revolt against Rome, with
1 Peter	destruction of the Temple in Jerusalem in 70
2 Peter	
1 John	
2 John	66–74 Gospel of Mark composed
3 John	
Jude	80–90 Gospels of Matthew and Luke, book of
Revelation	Acts composed
	100 Gospel of John composed

works, life, teachings, sacrifice, and Resurrection, as well as offer the first articulations of faith in Jesus as the Christ (the Greek equivalent of the Hebrew word *Messiah*, both of which mean "anointed"). They also laid the foundations for some churches' leadership structures (such as bishop, priest, and deacon) and offer moral instruction for Christian life. As such, the New Testament offers the essential foundation for Christian theology. Although much of Christian theology is postbiblical (meaning it developed after the writings of the New Testament), no defensible Christian theology can be abiblical (or unconcerned with the Bible as a foundation).

EARLY CHRISTIAN APOCRYPHA

There are more than thirty "gospel" accounts of the life of Jesus that did not make it into the canon of the New Testament. Similarly, numerous Christian epistles are not part of the New Testament. These writings that are not in the Bible were excluded because the dominant impulses within early Christian communities and church leaders found the excluded letters and gospels to be somehow false or untrue to their understanding of Jesus or correct Christian thinking. Many of these sources were suppressed or lost over the ages but have been recovered today through both accidental surfacing and scholarly research. Good academic resources for beginners studying the noncanonical (not included in the Bible) Jesus narratives include the following:

> Cameron, Ron, ed. *The Other Gospels: Non-Canonical Gospel Texts.* Philadelphia: Westminster, 1982.
>
> Ehrman, Bart D. *Lost Scriptures: Books That Did Not Make It into the New Testament.* New York: Oxford University Press, 2003.
>
> Elliott, J. K. *The Apocryphal New Testament: A Collection of Apocryphal Christian Literature in an English Translation.* Oxford, UK: Clarendon, 1993.

Palestine at the Time of Jesus

© 2009 ANSELM ACADEMIC

Sidon

Damascus

SYR

+ Mt. Hermon

Tyre

PHOENICIA

Caesarea Philippi

The Great Sea
(Mediterranean Sea)

GALILEE

Capernaum

Bethsaida

Magdala

Sea of
Galilee

Cana

Mt. Carmel +

Tiberias

Sepphoris

Nazareth

+ Mt. Tabor

Caesarea
Maritima

DECAPOLIS

SAMARIA

Jordan River

Mt. Gerizim

Sychar

+

Joppa

Arimathea?

PEREA

Emmaus?

Jericho

Jerusalem

+ Mt. Olives

Bethany

JUDEA

Salt
Sea
(Dead
Sea)

Hebron

0   20   40 miles

0   20   40 kilometers

IDUMEA

Scripture Scholarship

Although Christian theology relies on the Bible as a foundation, it cannot do so effectively without tools for reading and interpretation. The Bible may be revelation, but that claim alone does not guarantee that readers will understand the revelation it presents. To arrive at reasonable and responsible readings of the Bible, Christians require a biblical theology that helps them negotiate the panoply of interpretive challenges. The study of scriptural interpretation is called biblical hermeneutics (from the Greek *hermeneuein*, meaning "to translate or interpret"). This study comprises many distinct scholarly specializations, all of which aim at producing a responsible, historically conscious, critically astute approach to reading the Bible. Some of these specializations include manuscript evaluation, source criticism, form criticism, historical criticism, redaction criticism, rhetorical criticism, study of ancient languages, and study of different translations.

Manuscript evaluation is sometimes called lower criticism because it deals with the most basic task of arriving at clean and correct versions of the ancient manuscripts. Before word processing or even the printing press, people wrote by hand on fragile materials like clay and papyrus. These materials were subject to decay over time. Before biblical books can be read and interpreted today, the actual print text must first be determined by careful study of the manuscripts that have survived the ages.

Source criticism assumes that earlier written documents underlie the present form of the Bible. This theory resulted from the discovery of at least four authors behind the present version of the Pentateuch (the first five books of the Old Testament, long believed by many to have been singularly authored by the prophet Moses). When scholars studied these books carefully, they noticed things like different names for God, unique phrasing or emphases repeated at different points in the text, varying names for prominent geographical locations, and repetition of stories with slight differences. As researchers extracted, for example, all the passages that referred to God as *Yahweh* as opposed to *Elohim*, they discovered a whole perspective that was interwoven with other perspectives to create the version of the books that exists today. Source criticism is akin to searching for the bibliography behind the present biblical text. When scholars can locate the sources that comprise a biblical text, they are able to understand the different contexts and concerns of individual biblical authors.

Form criticism assumes that there are also oral and unwritten sources behind the present-day text. The effort to find specific sources, as described above, can be highly conjectural. Today, for example, scholars debate the four-source theory, not because they dispute that there were several authors of the Pentateuch, but because they disagree on exactly how many there were. Form criticism avoids the excesses and conjectural aspects of source criticism by focusing instead on the original meaning of individual units of the text. First, a selection of text is isolated and defined, and then the purpose and effect that the biblical material would have had on its original audiences is considered.

For example, form critics might examine the law code in the book of Exodus by asking who its audience was and how the book functioned in the ancient world, as opposed to asking what written sources contributed to its development. By such methods, researchers are able to arrive at responsible interpretations of challenging content.

Historical criticism considers the historical context of biblical writings. Scholars using this approach actively imagine and enter into the world of the text. They attempt to unveil sociopolitical realities that surrounded the writing of the Bible in order to distinguish between essential biblical content and inessential remnants of historical contingencies. Researchers also study historical context in order to assess what is likely or unlikely to have actually occurred.

For example, researchers studying the letters called the pastoral Epistles (1 and 2 Timothy, Titus) argue that although these letters are attributed to Paul, they cannot be so in fact. This is because the letters deal with the issues of false teachers and women's roles in the emergent church. In particular, the letters condemn false teachers who seem to be spreading a Gnostic form of Christianity that became popular in the late first century. Broadly understood, Gnostics belonged to one of a number of religious movements that claimed that salvation comes from secret knowledge available only to the elite initiated in that religion. These letters further demarcate limits for women's participation and leadership in the church, and a variety of indicators suggest that the move to restrict women's participation was also a development of the late first century. These two clues place the letter's time of writing at the end of the first century. Paul, however, is believed to have died closer to the middle of the first century (in the late 60s). A study of historical context reveals then that Paul cannot be the letters' author; rather, Paul's name was used as a tool by the actual author to gain credibility for the point of view espoused in the letters.

Redaction criticism investigates the historical editing of texts. Frequently, material is recounted in several places in the Bible, with minor differences and emphases. Often, thematic or tonal inconsistencies in biblical texts suggest that a number of documents were compiled and edited together to produce the text in its present form. By using redaction criticism, scholars can interpret why the same stories make multiple appearances in the Bible, why their authors interpret and relay them differently, and why there are inconsistencies in tone or theme.

For example, scholars studying Paul's correspondence with the church in Corinth (in 1 and 2 Corinthians) have been able to reconstruct a likely scenario about when Paul visited the church there, what happened during his visits to Corinth, and what specific issues were the occasion of his writing. Through scholarly re-creation of the historical context, researchers have been able to posit a plausible explanation for the radical difference in tone noticed respectively in chapters 1–9 and 10–13 of 2 Corinthians. Likely, these two sets of chapters were originally from two separate letters, later edited together to form the letter we now have.

Rhetorical criticism studies the effect of the texts as a whole. Scholars using this approach read the Bible, or segments of the Bible, as works of literature. By using rhetorical criticism, scholars are able to assess the cultural effect and value of the Bible from era to era.

For example, the book of Jonah in the Old Testament is a narrative tale about a prophet of Israel, sent to the enemy city of Nineveh to preach God's word. Jonah resists carrying out God's order because he does not want the enemy people of Nineveh to be saved. Jonah disobeys God by attempting to flee in the direction opposite to

Nineveh, but while he is onboard his escape ship, his treachery is revealed. The other sailors, fearing for their safety, toss him overboard, where Jonah is rescued in the belly of a large fish (the famed whale). Where does the fish take him? To Nineveh!

Often people ask historical questions of this story, such as, How can a man live inside a whale's stomach? or, Was there really a man named Jonah that had this incredible experience? Rhetorical criticism, by contrast, is interested in why such a story is in the Bible in the first place. What did its original readers learn from it? Scholars argue that this book was written in the 400s BCE, after the time the Israelite people had been exiled from the land of Israel in Palestine. The experience of exile and foreign occupation created in the Jewish people a fierce need to protect and preserve their cultural uniqueness. This need, however, was commonly acted out as intolerance of religious and ethnic differences. By placing the text of Jonah in its historical situation, modern readers can derive a richer awareness of the story's meaning for its original, Israelite audience. It was a comedic portrayal of an unruly prophet and a serious commentary on the universality of God's message that reaches even to one's enemies. Through rhetorical criticism, readers today can appreciate the story as the morality play that it was always intended to be.

Study of ancient languages enables scholars to read the Bible in its original languages, which are Hebrew, Aramaic, and Greek. Many scholars also study Latin because the Vulgate, the scholar Jerome's fifth-century Latin translation of the Greek and Hebrew biblical texts, was the standard Christian Bible in the West for more than a thousand years (being commonly used until the mid-sixteenth century).

Study of different translations of the Bible is an important component to being able to read scripture well. Translations from one language to another require the translator to make judgments about diction (word choice) and syntax (sentence structure). In this way, modern translators interpret the meaning of the original text for the general reader. Some translators attempt literal (or word-for-word equivalency) translations, while others attempt idiomatic (or common speech) renditions. Today there are dozens of different modern English translations of the Bible, produced and approved by various Christian communities. Learning the philosophies behind different translations and comparing modern versions of the Bible with one another, as well as with Greek and Hebrew versions, are valuable strategies that expand the contemporary reader's sense of the original text.

Tradition

Beyond church buildings and administrative structures, the Christian concept of church fundamentally refers to the collective body of Christian people. If all church buildings collapsed or governments prohibited people from worshipping in them, Christians could still *be* church with one another, provided they were authentic to their common faith. Great geographic distances, language barriers, cultures, customs, and even historical epochs may separate Christians (for *church* refers not only to living Christians but to all Christians throughout time). Still, people may be considered the church as long as they are connected by their authentic faith. Authentic faith is the cement that connects disparate peoples into one universal church, so Christians have a high stake in determining how and what makes their community a true expression of authentic Christian faith.

How do Christians determine the authenticity of their faith? At least in part, the answer is with tradition. The word *tradition* derives from the Latin root *tradere* meaning "to hand down." This etymology (or word history) is useful for pointing out that tradition is not a mystical way of blocking innovation. Much as family traditions are handed down, preserved, and shaped from one generation to the next (think of recipes, family heirlooms, and stories told at the holidays), so too does the faith tradition bear the fingerprints of history, embodying how people have long held and preserved their most sacred notions, relics, texts, and so on.

In the early Christian era, it was particularly difficult to establish what the tradition was, because it was just beginning to form. Because the Christian faith did not have thousands of years of precedents to call on in its first centuries, early Christians often found themselves embroiled in great debates about what they should believe and how they should state those beliefs. When disputes arose, people often claimed that their position was the traditional or original point of view. To defend their positions, they would cite passages from the Bible or letters written by other prominent Christians whose religious authority was considered beyond reproach. By claiming that certain beliefs were more ancient or widely held than others, Christian leaders and teachers established which were authentic. By the fifth century, theologians began to define authentic faith by the criteria of being believed everywhere, always, and by everyone; today, these criteria are called universality, antiquity, and consensus, respectively.

What actually comprises tradition for Christians? Some argue that Christian tradition refers exclusively to the Bible and its history of interpretation. Others hold that tradition may also include other elements, such as doctrinal statements, liturgical (or worship) practices, and even oral or informal Christian beliefs and practices. Still others hold that the Bible alone is authoritative, rejecting the authority of any other aspect of Christianity, including historical interpretation of the Bible.

Traditions Flowing from the Bible

Christians of the first several centuries spoke of tradition as it applied to biblical interpretation. When controversies arose, there were as yet no other widely acknowledged sources of authority, so people turned to the Bible. Over time, traditional ways of interpreting the Bible (especially problematic passages) were so often repeated they became the default position of the Christian community. For example, the Song of Songs is a wedding song that speaks poetically about the joys of marital lovemaking. Because of its sexual content, it would likely have been eliminated from the canon of the Bible had there not been a long tradition of interpreting the poem as an allegory for the love between God and his people. An allegorical interpretive tradition of this book of the Bible thus emerged and became the lens through which later generations typically interpreted the meaning of this book.

Faith was considered legitimate (or orthodox) when it conformed to the interpretive traditions that similarly emerged. It was considered false (or heresy) when inconsistent with the interpretive traditions. Consistency with the tradition of interpretation on the meaning of the Bible, dating back to the beginning of the Christian era, is considered a mark of authentic Christian faith even today. By contrast, if someone derives a newfangled meaning from the Bible (as cult leaders sometimes do), the Christian community at large is likely to deem the interpretation problematic because it stands in opposition to the biblical tradition.

Extrabiblical Tradition

From the beginning of the Christian movement, Christian thinkers grappled with an array of questions about belief and conduct about which the Bible did not provide clear or definitive instruction. An early example is the developing doctrine of the Trinity in the third and fourth centuries. The Bible speaks of Father, Son, and Spirit, but it does not explain in a clearly formulated doctrine what the relationship between Father, Son, and Spirit is. The Bible likewise speaks of the "Word becoming flesh," but it does not state in a formal doctrine what the relationship is between Jesus' human and divine natures. As Christian thinkers attempted to understand what the right way was for thinking about God from a Christian perspective, they developed a large body of writings (including treatises, argumentative papers and letters, and position papers formed by councils of church leaders). These and other writings about an array of topics and issues accumulated over time and eventually became a second source for later generations' thinking about the Christian faith tradition.

To use a more current example, the Bible speaks of the sanctity of marriage as the only location for moral sexual expression. It does not, however, comment on whether a married couple may use reproductive technologies such as in vitro fertilization to conceive a child or whether the couple has the right to determine their child's gender and so on. Because the Bible remains silent on an ever-growing number of questions, some Christians look to their church authorities as guarantors of authentic teaching. As churches produce official documents and dogmas (or official teachings), these materials become another source of authority that complements the revelation of the Bible.

Different Christian groups regard the idea of an extrabiblical source of authority varyingly, with some heartily rejecting the possibility and others warmly embracing it. For example, the Lutheran reformers of the sixteenth century championed the slogan *sola scriptura* ("the Bible alone"), whereas Roman Catholics then and now accept official church documents, such as papal encyclicals, creeds, and decrees produced by ecumenical councils, as authoritative.

Informal Tradition

Some Christians will distinguish between Tradition, with a capital *T*, and tradition, with a lowercase *t*. This is a useful, if imprecise, way of acknowledging that some elements of Christian tradition are more foundational than others. For example, the great tomes of systematic theology, developed by thinkers such as Thomas Aquinas or Bonaventure, are more often sources for contemporary Christian thought than the obscure poetry of anonymous medieval monks. Formal church services often mimic practices that have endured for most of Christianity's two-thousand-year history, while homespun practices such as making advent wreaths with one's children come in and out of vogue. Essential elements of the Christian tradition manifest a self-evident authority. Other elements of the tradition are more obviously matters of taste and aesthetic and hence lack authority even while they remain sources of the tradition. Such elements might include the following:

- prayers
- worship styles
- vestments (religious garments)
- spiritual and devotional practices, such as going on pilgrimage, fasting, or meditating
- written works, such as collections of prayers or works of theology

Church authorities largely determine the content of the authoritative Christian tradition, but in the end, it is the *sensus fidelium* ("the sense of the faithful") that has the last word. The church is the people, and what the people deem authentic in each era is ultimately what comprises the Christian faith for every generation.

Reason

In a fundamental sense, human reason must be a source or foundation for Christian theology. Through reason, people are able to acquire knowledge and form conclusions, judgments, or inferences.

Christian faith thus assumes that reason is necessary to the theological task, but there are questions about the role and extent of its use. Emerging from the Christian claim that God reveals Godself, the questions of reason in theology become as follows: What is the relationship between reason and revelation? Is reason enough? Is revelation enough?

What is the relationship between reason and revelation? This basic question recognizes the relationship between these two sources of knowledge. Theology has classically incorporated the tools of reason (such as logical deduction, proofs for validity, postulates, and conclusions) into its systematic thinking. In this sense, reason may be understood as a tool that theology uses to unpack the content it receives from God's revelation. For example, theologians ask questions such as, If God is all powerful and all merciful, why does God allow people to suffer? This question reflects what at first glance appears to be an illogical Christian claim that God is both powerful and merciful and yet God allows people to suffer. Christians would use rational argumentation, in this instance, to demonstrate logically that God's power and mercy can exist simultaneously with human suffering. The basic relationship between reason and revelation is functional, with reason acting as a tool, or a "handmaid," for explicating the mysteries of Christian faith.

Is reason enough? Another perspective is that reason need not be seen as a handmaid to theology. The idea is that whatever people need to know is available to them through their philosophical investigation and observation of nature. Even though religious faith may complement what is known by reason, it is not necessary for the rational person. Moreover, religious faith can never trump reason, because reason serves as the judge of religious claims. This position characterized the Enlightenment, an eighteenth-century intellectual movement in Europe and America, which believed reason to be omnicompetent (totally capable) in discerning truth. Enlightenment thinkers were highly critical of Christian truth claims and accepted Christian theology only to the extent that it could be deemed rational. Seemingly irrational claims, such as the belief in miracles or Jesus' Resurrection from the dead, were dismissed as superstitious. Rationally tenable claims, such as Jesus' teachings in the Sermon on the Mount (a famous series of lessons in the Gospel of Matthew), were maintained. Here the relationship between revelation and reason is one of critique, with reason judging what is religiously admissible.

Is revelation enough? A third perspective is that revelation, and not reason, has the final say in matters of human knowing. Although privileging reason is attractive, reason itself does not speak to all aspects of human thought. There are affective (pertaining to the emotions or sentiment) dimensions of knowing that seem to defy reason's ability to describe or contain. To the extent that theology as interpreter of revelation deals with affective dimensions and responses of knowing, including beauty, love, friendship, and so on, it supersedes reason. Christians often speak of the mysteries of their faith, by which they refer to aspects beyond rational description. In these instances, revelation is more abundant than reason. The relationship between revelation and reason is one of transcendence, with revelation simultaneously encompassing and surpassing all that is rationally knowable.

The dialogue between Christianity and philosophy is as old as Christian history. It represents Christian theology's practice of looking toward reason as a source for its own discernment of truth. Although there is no absolute consensus on the relationship between Christian theology and philosophy, their inevitable dialogue demonstrates the timeless foundation of reason for the theological enterprise.

Experience

Theology is rooted in human experience. On some level theology cannot be detached from human experience, because doing theology is itself a human endeavor. However, good theology must self-consciously pay attention to lived experience as a source and judge of truth if it wants to remain authentic, relevant, and vital to people's lives. Experience, in Christian understanding, may be thought of as a source and a gauge for truth, as an interpretive framework, and as establishing a hermeneutical circle of theory and praxis.

A Source of Truth

How is lived experience a source of truth? One could argue that experience carries truth within itself, almost as a type of revelation. Often, truth gleaned from experience is more powerful than truth learned in a book or a classroom. In fifth-grade health class, for example, children can learn about human reproduction, and in eighth-grade home economics, children can simulate the experience of caring for a baby by carrying around a bag of flour for a day. Although possibly useful on some level, no such lessons can really prepare people for the experience of parenthood. Being a parent is itself a form of schooling in which patience, forgiveness, leadership, discipline, nutrition, and so on are daily lessons. The experience of parenting teaches one how to parent in a way that no merely theoretical approach can.

In a similar manner, experience is a touchstone for theology. Christian doctrine and the Bible may speak about love, justice, forgiveness, redemption, and so on. The reality of these truths, however, is borne out in experiences that teach people these truths by way of living them. Experience is a source that gives rise to insight and also conditions theoretical knowledge with the wisdom of "having been there." Moreover, the recognition that human experience is a foundation for Christian theology enables theology to speak for and out of human experience in general. In other words, Christian theology is not only interested in how Christians believe and behave. It is also interested in human life as a whole.

A Gauge for Truth

When theology speaks meaningfully to lived experience, it becomes a vital tool for the application of faith in daily life. On the other hand, when theology makes claims that do not resonate with people's lived experience, it risks being discounted as irrelevant at best and dangerous at worst. Experience serves as a gauge for determining whether religious truth claims are adequate and authentic.

Another example may be helpful. For the better part of Christian history, celibate (or nonsexually active and unmarried) clergymen produced the dominant works of theology. Nevertheless, marriage, sexuality, and family issues featured prominently among the topics of their investigations. One can find many negative statements on sexuality and marriage from Christian theologians of past eras. Unsurprisingly, these negative views often were posited by individuals who saw their celibate lifestyle as superior to married life. Today, theology is more "democratic," both in its views and in the scope of its authors. Married persons reading negative comments from the past about marriage recognize a disconnect between their own lived experience and the words of those who spoke about, but did not experience, marriage. Trusting more in the truth derived from married life, people today widely discount the negative views of the past in favor of contemporary voices that celebrate marriage and family as venerable expressions of Christian living. Across a wide range of theological concerns, experience serves as a gauge to keep theological claims honest and true to people's lives.

An Interpretive Framework

Lived experience, beyond serving as a source and gauge of theology, also relates to Christian theology in the sense that human experience needs to be interpreted. Human experience is often ambiguous. People question the origin, purpose, and destiny of their lives and of collective human experience: What do we know? How do we know it? Why do we exist at all? These perennial questions derive from reflecting on our experience. Christian theology provides a framework for interpreting experience. Indeed, at base, the purpose of Christian theology is to provide a framework for making sense of human life. Moreover, having a faith-based, interpretive framework for life helps people avoid an exaggerated sense of individualism and the attitude "anything goes as long as I like it," so common in contemporary, industrialized cultures. In this way, experience not only gauges theological adequacy, it also is gauged itself.

The Hermeneutical Circle of Theory and Praxis

This dialogue between theology and experience may be more closely examined as the intersection between theory and praxis. *Theory* describes the theoretical component of theology, for theology could also be loosely described as "religious theories about human life." *Praxis* refers to intentional, reflective action that is driven by theory. For example, one may theorize that she will find more meaning in life by helping others, but it is praxis when one subsequently volunteers at a women's shelter on the basis of her theory.

The relationship between theory and praxis is sometimes called a hermeneutical circle. *Hermeneutics* in this context means "self-conscious interpretation of theory." Frequently used to describe interpretation of the Bible, hermeneutics may also more broadly be understood as an interpretive theological approach that connects theory and reflective action. In his work *Theology of Liberation*, Gustavo Gutierrez argues that theology rises only at sundown. This colorful image communicates the basic point that Christian faith is mostly about lived, day-to-day experience. At sundown, after the day's work, it makes sense to theorize and reflect on the day's lessons and value. The evening reflection may shed new insight on how to act tomorrow. This creates a circular pattern of doing, reflecting, revising action, reflecting further, and so on.

The model of the hermeneutical circle captures the indelible connection between experience and theology. Theology must begin in people's lives and return its reflective insights back to people's lives. Experience is an inescapable source for insight and authenticity in Christian thought.

Conclusion

Christian thought is immersed in history, in the world, and in people's experiences. Christian thought is dialogical and developmental and uses classical sources from its tradition, as well as contemporary insights drawn from nearly every discipline of study and every walk of life. The four foundations of Christian thought considered in this chapter illustrate the interplay between the past and present, the tradition and lived experience, reason and faith, and the Bible and its interpretation.

Questions for Discussion and Review

1. Name and describe the four sources or foundations of Christian theology. Can you identify any ways in which they intersect or overlap?

2. Differentiate between the Old and New Testaments.

3. Name and differentiate types of scholarly criticism of the Bible.

4. How are the books of the Old and New Testaments respectively grouped?

5. Describe the role of tradition in Christian theology. How would you differentiate between formal and informal aspects of this tradition?

6. What are the possible relationship models between reason and revelation in Christian theology? Which model makes the most sense to you, and why?

7. How is experience both a source and a gauge for theological insight?

8. Describe the hermeneutical circle. How does theory inform action, and conversely, how does action inform theory?

Key Terms

affective

apocalyptic

Apocrypha

canon

celibate

First and Second
  Testaments

Hebrew Bible

hermeneutics

record of revelation

Resurrection

revelation

sensus fidelium

Septuagint

Sermon on the
  Mount

Tanakh

Resources

Albl, Martin C. *Reason, Faith, and Tradition: Explorations in Catholic Theology.* Winona, MN: Anselm Academic, 2009.

Bonsor, Jack A. *Athens and Jerusalem: The Role of Philosophy in Theology.* Eugene, OR: Wipf & Stock, 2003.

Gelpi, Donald. *The Turn to Experience in Contemporary Theology.* Mahwah, NJ: Paulist Press, 1994.

Sokolowski, Robert. *The God of Faith and Reason: Foundations of Christian Theology.* Washington, DC: Catholic University Press, 1995.

3 Periods in Christian History

WHAT TO EXPECT

This chapter is a basic introduction to the major historical divisions in Christian thought. It discusses the following key periods:

- the biblical era, 2000 BCE–100 CE
- the patristic era, 100–700
- the Middle Ages, 700–1500
- the Reformation, 1500–1750
- the modern era, 1750–present

The Biblical Era

The biblical era of Christian thought has two major divisions: the Old Testament period and the New Testament period. Together these periods constitute the principal foundation for Christian thought and are frequently consulted and referred to by Christian theologians. The main textual materials that come from these periods are the books of the Old and New Testaments. Noncanonical books, as well as materials from neighboring cultures of the Ancient Near East, archaeological discoveries, and artifacts are also useful tools for understanding the history of these eras.

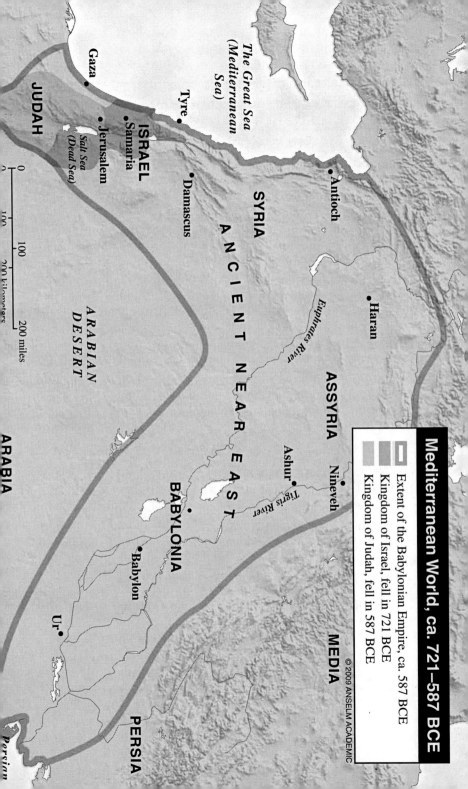

Mediterranean World, ca. 721–587 BCE

Extent of the Babylonian Empire, ca. 587 BCE
Kingdom of Israel, fell in 721 BCE
Kingdom of Judah, fell in 587 BCE

© 2009 ANSELM ACADEMIC

TIME LINE OF ANCIENT CULTURES

3150 BCE	Early Bronze Age
ca. 3100	First Egyptian dynasty
3000	Birth of the Sumerian culture
2575–2150	Age of the pyramids at Giza
ca. 2000	Civilization of Minoans in Crete
ca. 1700	Hammurabi establishes law code in Babylon
ca. 1250	Israel's Exodus from Egypt
ca. 1200	Beginning of the Iron Age
1200	Trojan War
1000	Beginning of the Kingdom of Israel
ca. 850	Life of Greek poet Homer
780	Settlement of Greek colonies throughout Asia Minor
753	Founding of Rome
722	Assyrian Empire defeats Kingdom of Israel
660s	Twenty-sixth Egyptian dynasty
594	Solon reforms the harsh law code for Athens
587	Judah is exiled to Babylon under Nebuchadnezzar
563–483	Life of Buddha
551–478	Life of Confucius
492–449	Persian Wars
431–404	Peloponnesian War
427–347	Life of Plato
384–322	Life of Aristotle
356–323	Life of Alexander the Great
264–241; 218–202; 149–146	Punic Wars and Roman domination of the Mediterranean
221	Start of construction of the Great Wall of China
167–142	Maccabean revolt against Seleucid rulers of Palestine
142–63	Hasmonean rule in Palestine

Continued

Continued	
63	Roman general Pompey conquers Palestine
44	Assassination of Julius Caesar
4 BCE–30 CE	Life of Jesus
37–100	Life of Jewish historian Josephus
66–70	First Jewish revolt and the destruction of the Jewish Temple in Jerusalem
64; 90–96; 98–117	First three notable Roman persecutions of Christians
132–135	Second Jewish revolt
272–337	Life of Constantine the Great
325	First Christian council in Nicaea

The Old Testament Period

Christians divide the Old Testament period into several important historical moments BCE, as follows:

2000–1500: The first subdivision of the Old Testament period is the era of the great patriarchs, such as Abraham, Isaac, Jacob, and Joseph. This was also the time that the tribes of Israel were forming. During this period, the Israelites were seminomadic herders who migrated throughout the Fertile Crescent to pasture and water their flocks.

1500–1250: The Hebrews (later known as the Israelites) lived in Egypt. How many Hebrews lived in Egypt and how long they lived there is a matter of scholarly debate. The biblical record highlights three aspects of Israelite life during this period: their numbers increased significantly, they were enslaved and treated harshly by the Egyptian pharaoh, and they were led by God through the prophet Moses to freedom. This last event, known as the Exodus, became the central unifying story for the tribes of Israel in the centuries that followed.

1250–1020: The Israelites settled into the land of Canaan, where they lived under the rule of tribal leaders, called judges. Archaeological evidence suggests that many of the groups that later identified themselves as Israelites were native to Canaan. In other words, some of the people later considered Israelite were already living in Canaan when the freed slaves migrated there from Egypt. There are also inconsistencies between the biblical description of how Canaan was settled (in the books of Joshua and Judges) and what the archaeological record indicates. Some evidence points toward Israelite conquest (as in the book of Joshua), but other evidence suggests a more peaceful, long-term, mutual enculturation between Canaanites and Israelites, punctuated by infighting and tension among tribes (as in the book of Judges).

1020–930: The tribes of Israel decided to form a federation led by a king. The biblical record indicates a mixed attitude concerning the risks and benefits of having a king (especially in 1 Samuel). Three kings reigned over the united Israelite tribes: Saul, David, and Solomon. Among the highlights in the biblical account of this era was the construction of the Temple in Jerusalem during the reign of Solomon.

930–722: The Kingdom of Israel is divided. After the death of Solomon, ten tribes in the north elected an independent king and established independent shrines for worship at the key sites of Dan and Bethel. The Bible indicates that the ten tribes separated from the southern king due to overtaxation and being forced to provide labor for the king. The northern tribes concluded that "they had no share" in the kingdom of the south (see 1 Kings chapter 12). The history of the division of the kingdom into the northern kingdom of Israel and the southern kingdom of Judah (replete with the stories of the kings who reigned in each region) may be found in the books of 1 and 2 Kings. The northern kingdom of Israel was destroyed by the Assyrians in 722. Israelites were torn from their homes and forcibly relocated, causing the Diaspora (or scattering) of Hebrew persons and culture throughout the ancient Near East (see 2 Kings chapter 17).

930–587: The remaining southern tribes of Judah and Benjamin continued their kingdom of Judah during this period, maintaining a capital in Jerusalem and leadership under the dynasty of

David. The kingdom of Judah was destroyed by the Babylonians in 587 (see 2 Kings chapter 25). (See map, Mediterranean World, ca. 721–587 BCE.)

587–539: Following the Babylonian conquest of the kingdom of Judah, some Israelites were allowed to remain to tend the land, but most professionals and individuals of high birth were forcibly relocated to Babylon. This event, called the Babylonian Exile, constituted a major alteration in Israelite culture, principally because the people lost the land they believed God had promised them. Without this land, Israel turned to its oral and written traditions to preserve its culture. Much of the Bible was developed during the Exile.

539–425: Babylonian forces that had once conquered Israel were themselves conquered by the Persian king Cyrus the Great. Cyrus allowed those who had been forcibly relocated to Babylon to return to their homelands, under the rule of Persian-approved governors. The Israelites were thus permitted to return to Jerusalem to rebuild the city and restore their culture.

425–333: The Israelites lived under relatively peaceful Persian rule.

333–175: The restored Jews living as a vassal kingdom of Persia (meaning they were allowed to keep their land in return for homage, loyalty, and taxes paid to their overlords) were once again conquered. Under the tactical genius of Alexander the Great, Greek forces overwhelmed Palestine. This period was tumultuous and oppressive for the Jews, especially under the cruel rule of Antioch Epiphanes in the second century BCE. Brutality, religious oppression, and the cultural transformations that resulted from centuries of occupation led Jews of this era to ask how best to preserve their faith and culture. Different responses to this question resulted in the emergence of various sects within Judaism, including the Pharisees, Sadducees, and resistance movements (all of whom are mentioned in the New Testament).

175–64: The Jews organized a revolt, led by Judas Maccabeus, to throw off their oppressors. The Maccabean revolt led to a period of Jewish independence and the establishment of the Hasmonean

Dynasty. During this era, the final books of the Old Testament were composed. The years between the close of the Old Testament writings and the beginning of the New Testament writings is known as the intertestamental period.

The New Testament Period

The New Testament period is much briefer than the Old Testament period, spanning roughly one hundred years. It marks not only a change in historical context but also, and perhaps more important, a change in perspective about the meaning of Israel's history, as well as a change in the ethnic and cultural vantage point of the New Testament authors. The events of the life of Jesus occur in Roman-occupied Judea, covering the territory between Galilee in the north to Jerusalem in the south. Jesus' life spanned roughly 4 BCE to 30 CE, during which time the political situation was highly tumultuous.

The Roman general Pompey had conquered Jerusalem in 63 BCE. Jewish autonomy was seriously curtailed under this new Roman rule. The Romans appointed Herod (descended from the Jewish Hasmonean Dynasty) as king to rule over Judea. However, Herod remained under Roman control. He reigned from 37 BCE until his death in 4 BCE. After Herod's death, Judea was ruled directly by Roman governors, without mediation from a Roman-appointed Hasmonean king. This was an oppressive situation for the Jews, who resisted Roman rule and revolted sporadically throughout the first century.

A widespread revolt occurred in 66 CE, which ended in the destruction of Jerusalem and ruination of the Temple. The Jewish historian Josephus records massive Jewish casualties during this uprising. A Jewish high court, or sanhedrin, reconvened in the city of Javneh in 70 CE. Over the next several decades, Jewish communities stabilized throughout the Roman Empire. Jewish religious and communal life, however, no longer had the Jerusalem Temple and its priests as its central focus. Religious life relocated its emphasis to rabbis, study of the Torah, and the communal gathering in synagogues. Life for Jews and the Jewish offshoot sect that would eventually be called Christianity was perilous throughout the first century and beyond.

The life of Jesus and the birth of the early Christian church occurred in this sometimes violent and always oppressive context of Roman occupation. Much of the apocalyptic (or "end-of-the-world") thinking found in both the teachings of Jesus and the beliefs of the early Christians can be attributed to this context, which was brimming with injustice, vulnerability for the occupied people, and hope for deliverance. People could be seized from their homes and forced into labor, women and girls suffered sexual violence at the hands of the Roman military, and people were heavily taxed at an unsustainable rate.

The emerging Christian community and the development of the Christian New Testament must be understood against this violent colonial backdrop. Among the tensions and conflicts underlying the burgeoning Jesus movement were the following issues and questions:

What was the nature of the Messiah? Jews had long hoped for deliverance from occupation and restoration of their kingdom. The prophetic writings from the period during and after the Babylonian Exile imagine a free and flourishing Jewish kingdom, in which both the northern and southern tribes are reunited and stronger than ever (for example, see Ezekiel chapter 37). Many Jews expected a Messiah (or anointed king) to be the catalyst and leader of this new golden age. By the time of the New Testament writings, which began to be developed in the middle of the first century CE, followers of the Jesus movement were identifying Jesus by the term *Messiah*. The problem, however, was that the Jewish homelands were still occupied by the Romans, and the Jewish kingdom had not been restored. The issue forced the Jews to question the nature and role of the expected Messiah. Was he to be a temporal, political figure who would deliver the Jews from oppressive Roman rule, or was the Messiah an apocalyptic figure who would usher in a new age? In short, was Jesus indeed the Messiah of Jewish ancestral hope? Some Jews said yes, becoming the first Christians; others said no, stringently opposing the first Christians.

What was the relationship between Judaism and the Jesus movement? Because Jesus and his followers were themselves Jewish, the original Christians were actually Jews. This fact led to one of the most challenging issues for the New Testament community. Jewish followers of Jesus and Jewish opponents of Jesus are seen in the New

Testament as vying against one another over important claims, including the meaning of Messiah, the meaning of past Hebrew prophesies, and the interpretation of Hebrew texts (i.e., the Old Testament writings). There is a sense, moreover, in some of the New Testament writings (for example, the Letter to the Hebrews) that Christians, who themselves were experiencing hardships and disappointment as they waited to experience any benefit from their Christian beliefs, were tempted to convert back to Judaism. Furthermore, the Jesus movement was originally a Jewish movement, but it quickly became attractive to non-Jewish converts. These Gentile converts were interested in the benefits of the Jewish/Christian God but did not want to follow the rigorous Jewish Law. As more and more Greeks and Romans became Christians, distance grew between the Jesus movement and its roots in Judaism, putting Christians at even greater pains to prove themselves legitimate heirs to the Jewish heritage.

What was the relationship between Gentiles and the Jesus movement? It was not clear from the outset of the Jesus movement whether the Jewish Law was binding for Christians. Jewish followers of Jesus continued to observe the Law, and many key leaders of the emerging church apparently felt that all Christians needed to become Jewish before they could become Christian. This tension permeates the letters written by Paul (for example, the Letter to the Galatians), where there was open debate over whether Jewish Christians and non-Jewish Christians could share the Christian ritual meal together, because Jewish Law forbade the practice of Jews eating with non-Jews. Huge debate within the early Christian church centered on such questions as, Who can follow Jesus and be baptized into the Christian community? Can only ethnic and religious Jews become members of the community, or can Greeks and Romans also join? If Gentiles become Christians, must they also follow the Law and religious practices of Judaism?

How should the Jesus movement move into the future? After the death of Jesus and the first apostles (followers of the movement who spread Jesus' teachings after his death), questions arose about the nature and structure of the Christian community. Almost immediately there was rivalry among Jesus' closest friends about who should lead the new movement and what the movement should look like. What is more, the Apostle Paul did not know Jesus in life. Paul knew

Jesus only through a conversion experience brought about by Paul's encounter with the risen Jesus (see Acts chapters 9, 22, and 26). Paul is often depicted in his New Testament letters as struggling against Jesus' intimates over proper teachings about belief and conduct. In the absence of Jesus himself, early leaders of the Jesus movement had to deal with such questions as: Who should guide the church? How should disputes be settled when they arise? What are the official beliefs of the community?

These questions, among many others, reveal the uncertainty of the early Christian period. Against a backdrop of political oppression, cultural cross-pollination, and doctrinal development, the emergent Christian community navigated issues of identity, political persecution, civic responsibility, group organization, and future sustainability. These concerns largely directed the historical development of Christian thought in the following centuries.

The Patristic Era

The patristic era (derived from the Latin *pater*, meaning "father"), typically refers to the period between 100 and 700. In this era, Christianity spread from its original location in Palestine throughout neighboring regions of the Roman Empire. The spread of Christianity included both geographical and ideological expansion, as this once-Jewish movement became thoroughly entrenched and informed by elements of the broader Greco-Roman culture. Key aspects to consider in this historical period include significant persons and places, major doctrinal developments, and conciliar outcomes of doctrinal debates.

Significant Persons and Places

Christian ideas spread beyond Jerusalem and the region of Palestine through the missionary efforts of early Christians. The New Testament records in detail, for example, the missionary work of the Apostle Paul. Paul's activities give us insight into the nature of the spread of the early Christian community. Missionaries would go alone or in

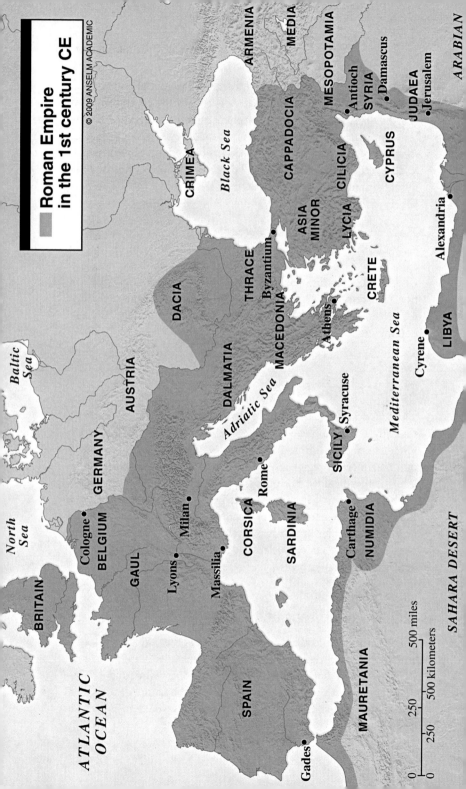

Roman Empire
in the 1st century CE
© 2009 ANSELM ACADEMIC

ARMENIA
MEDIA
MESOPOTAMIA
Damascus
Antioch
SYRIA
JUDAEA
Jerusalem
ARABIAN
CAPPADOCIA
CILICIA
CYPRUS
LYCIA
ASIA
MINOR
Alexandria
CRIMEA
Black Sea
CRETE
THRACE
Byzantium
DACIA
LIBYA
Cyrene
MACEDONIA
Athens
DALMATIA
Mediterranean Sea
AUSTRIA
Adriatic Sea
Baltic
Sea
SICILY
Syracuse
GERMANY
Rome
CORSICA
Carthage
NUMIDIA
Milan
BELGIUM
Cologne
SARDINIA
North
Sea
GAUL
Lyons
Massilia
BRITAIN
ATLANTIC
OCEAN
SPAIN
MAURETANIA
SAHARA DESERT
Gades

0   250   500 miles
0   250   500 kilometers

small groups to a new location, where they would take up work and residency while sharing the "good news" about Jesus. Once a community of believers was established, the missionary would move on to a new location, staying in touch via letters and occasional visits. The letters of the New Testament represent the correspondence among early Christian communities.

Christian missionaries expanded the reach of the new movement throughout North Africa, the Mediterranean area, and eastern Europe. A number of hub cities beyond Jerusalem and Rome became important locations for Christian theological development. Among the most important were Antioch (in modern-day Turkey), Alexandria (in modern-day Egypt), and Carthage (in modern-day Algeria).

Antioch was a principal location to which the Christian community fled following the fall of Jerusalem in 70. It produced a distinctive brand of theology, called Antiochene, characterized by its emphasis on the humanity of Jesus and its literal interpretation of the Bible. Major thinkers associated with Antioch include Basil the Great (ca. 330–379), Gregory of Nyssa (ca. 335–385), and Gregory of Nazianzus (ca. 330–389). These fourth-century theologians are collectively referred to as the Cappadocian fathers.

From the city of Alexandria came Alexandrian theology, which served as the foremost rival to the Antiochene approach. Deeply rooted in Greek philosophy, especially that of Plato, Alexandrian theology emphasized the divinity of Christ and the allegorical, or symbolic, interpretation of the Bible. Key thinkers associated with Alexandria include Clement of Alexandria (ca. 150–215), Origen (ca. 185–251), and Athanasius (ca. 293–373).

Carthage was a third city crucial to the developing Christian communities of the patristic era. Located in North Africa, Carthage was an important center for commerce and culture. It was distinctive in its theological approach, in part because Latin, rather than Greek, as elsewhere, was the dominant language of the region. A more legalistic approach to developing doctrine and Christian terminology characterized the theology. Key thinkers associated with Carthage include Tertullian (ca. 160–220), Cyprian of Carthage (third century; Cyprian's birth and death dates are unclear), and Augustine of Hippo (354–430), whose influence and range make him one of the most important theologians of the patristic era.

Major Doctrinal Developments

Numerous factors can be identified as root causes of doctrinal conflict and development in the patristic era. Persecution of Christians under Roman emperors, for example, left communities divided over what to do with repentant Christians who had renounced their faith under threat of physical torture. Should they be readmitted to Christian worship? If so, ought the community impose penalties on them? Diverse cultures and languages, as another example, often led devout believers to different conclusions regarding questions of faith. Greek-speaking Christians in Antioch held worldviews and ideas that varied from their counterparts in Alexandria and Latin-speaking Carthage (just as today residents of New York City, Paris, and London have different languages, cultures, manners, and so on). As a third example, the Hebraic roots of Christian thought differed dramatically from the worldviews expressed in Greco-Roman traditions. In particular, Hebraic thought argued for strict monotheism (one God), whereas pagan religion was polytheistic (plural gods). Christians came from both backgrounds, and such different starting points led to confusion when Christians asked questions about the relationship of Jesus to God and the Holy Spirit. (Were they one God? Two gods? Three gods?) These and other such factors resulted in many heated debates in the patristic era. Because there was no official church teaching and only limited historical precedent, these debates constituted the beginning of the development of Christian doctrine.

Following are some of the principal subjects of these debates:

- the structure of the church, the role of bishops, how authority was to be passed down, and the primacy of the Bishop of Rome (i.e., the pope)
- the selection of books to be included in the New Testament
- the role of tradition versus novel developments and ongoing "revelations" of the Holy Spirit, giving rise to heresies such as Montanism (a belief that new prophets and prophesies were revealed by the Holy Spirit even after the time of Jesus and the close of the New Testament writings) and Gnosticism (a variety of beliefs in elaborate hierarchies of divine beings)

- the nature of Christ, especially the relationship of his humanity to his divinity (which gave rise to the heresies of Nestorianism and Apollinarianism)

- the relationship among the Father, the Son, and the Holy Spirit in the Christian conception of God (which was the subject of the Arian controversy)

- the relationship with Christians who renounced Christ under persecution but wanted to return to the church after the persecution ended, giving rise to the Donatist controversy, whose proponents declined to forgive church leaders who had buckled under persecution. Donatists rejected the reinstatement of fallen priests and bishops, as well as the validity of sacraments (e.g., baptism) that such "apostate" priests and bishops had formerly celebrated.

- the role of grace versus free will in human salvation. This gave rise to the Pelagian controversy, in which different factions debated the extent to which the human will has freedom, apart from divine grace, to do good works.

Conciliar Outcomes of Doctrinal Debates

The patristic era of Christian thought must be understood against the changing background of Roman political life. Roman emperors throughout the first two centuries after Jesus' death were largely ambivalent about Christians. The Roman leadership was fairly tolerant of the budding Christian population, especially on account of Christians' notable public works and charities. However, Christians were required, with everyone else, to pay regular worship to the Roman emperor. When Christians refused on the grounds of religious belief, they risked persecution and even martyrdom. Christians were thus at pains to demonstrate to their rulers that they were good, upstanding citizens. They produced many works of classical apologia (or defenses of Christian practice and belief) on behalf of the Christian faith, a number of which survive today and tell us what life for Christians was once like. Despite these efforts, Christians were often a marginalized and at-risk population from the start of the movement until the beginning of the fourth century.

This situation changed due to the dramatic conversion to Christian faith by Emperor Constantine (ca. 272–337) in the fourth century. Historians debate whether Constantine's conversion was driven by religious or political motives, but the effect of his conversion was great. In 313 he issued the Edict of Milan, which officially required the toleration of Christianity, making Christianity a legitimate and protected religion in the empire. Christianity became the official religion of the Roman Empire under Emperor Theodosius (379–395) seven decades later. Constantine's effect on this era cannot be overstated, as he reversed the fortunes of Christianity from an oft-persecuted sect to the official religion of the Roman Empire.

Constantine's successor Theodosius confirmed Christianity as the state religion of Rome. This official status led to many changes: Christian holidays became part of the calendar; Christian churches were erected; persecution of Christians ended; church worship became formalized, with the inclusion of pagan customs; and priests and bishops received special social status. Also Constantine moved the seat of his empire from Rome to Constantinople (modern Istanbul), which gave rise to later power struggles between the church establishments located in both cities. In addition, with the emergent institutionalization of the church came a need to formalize Christian doctrine and settle tense doctrinal disputes. Throughout the third through eighth centuries, Christians met in councils to sort out conflicts of belief, organization, and leadership. Key councils of this era, and the central doctrinal outcomes they arrived at, include the following:

- The Council of Nicaea (325) arrived at the teaching that Jesus was of the same substance as the Father, and it produced the Nicene Creed. This council also helped to settle the Arian controversy, wherein some argued that Jesus was "created" rather than "eternally begotten."
- The Council of Constantinople (381) taught that Jesus had a human soul, as opposed to Apollinarian theories that held that Jesus' soul was the Holy Spirit.
- The Council of Ephesus (431) affirmed that there is only one person in Jesus. This was helpful in dispelling the Nestorian claim that there were two persons (one human and one divine inhabiting the same body) in Jesus and the Apollinarian claim that Christ had no human soul.

- The First Council of Chalcedon (451) concluded that there are two unconfused and undivided natures (human and divine) in one divine person in Christ, dispelling the Monophysite heresy, which argued that Christ had only one divine nature and no human nature.
- The Second Council of Constantinople (553) reaffirmed the teaching of the First Council of Chalcedon.
- The Third Council of Constantinople (681) taught that just as there is a human and divine nature in Christ, so also is there a human and divine will in Christ. This position contrasted with Monothelitism, whose proponents argued that Christ had only a divine will and no human will.

The Middle Ages

From the perspective of a history of Christian thought, it is helpful to subdivide the Middle Ages into the early Middle Ages (700–1000), the High Middle Ages (1000–2000), and the Renaissance or late Middle Ages (1300–1450). Any survey of historical periods is somewhat arbitrary. As with most eras, there are no absolute dates for the start and end of the Middle Ages.[1] However, it is useful to use the rough timeframes above, because they correspond to changes that occurred in the life of the church.

---

[1] Although the Middle Ages span roughly 700 to 1500, some will place the opening date of the Middle Ages as early as the year 410, when Rome was sacked by invading Northern European tribes. This signified for many the beginning of the end of the Roman Empire. By the end of the fifth century, the political stability of the Roman Empire had been replaced by the militaristic and feudal system of these conquering tribes. The introduction of their Germanic culture resulted in what is called the "Germanization" of the church.

Many conquering peoples became Christian, bringing with them new customs and values that influenced Christian practice and belief at the popular level. In a more formal way, churches were influenced because their control shifted from the bishops to the feudal lords. Conflict thus arose over who had the authority to name church clergy and leaders—kings or church leaders? This era classically has been referred to as the Dark Ages because of the fall of the Roman Empire. Many consider the Dark Ages to be the early Middle Ages (lasting from about 410 to 700). Nevertheless, because much of the patristic literature and conciliar activity were still developing at this time, these years can also easily be categorized as part of the patristic era.

Early Middle Ages

Several key developments shaped the landscape of Christian thought in this era. First, the religion of Islam (which started about 622) began to spread throughout North Africa and into Europe, eventually overtaking Constantinople itself. Second, regular fighting among feudal lords resulted in political instability throughout Western Europe. Third, to facilitate stability, garner protection, and gain political power, numerous Christian bishops consecrated or crowned kings. By doing so, they also directed who would be the "legitimate" lord of the land and claimed for the church the power to determine who would rule. A dramatic example of this occurred when Pope Leo III crowned Charlemagne as Holy Roman Emperor on Christmas Day in 800. In this role, Charlemagne's job was to spread and protect Christian worship and practice throughout Europe, which he did with great success. This close relationship between the papacy (the office of the pope of Rome) and the political rulers of Europe, however, proved the cause of much corruption in later generations.

High Middle Ages

By the eleventh century, Christian culture predominated throughout Western Europe. Monastic orders, begun in the patristic era, had become important social institutions and leading centers for the preservation and development of Christian theology. Known for its distinctive, highly ordered style of argumentation, theology of this era is referred to as "medieval" or "scholastic." Among the most important exemplars of scholastic theology is the corpus of Thomas Aquinas (1225–1274). Monastic orders were also important centers for moral reform, especially when the church became too politically inclined or corrupt. Among the most important reformers was Pope Gregory VII (reigned 1073–1085). His "Gregorian reform" spread canon law (or church law) throughout Europe and claimed for the pope the highest spiritual authority.

Bleaker features of this age include the Crusades (1095–1204), a series of military campaigns in which Christian armies sought to reclaim formerly Christian lands from Islamic rule. Moreover, a long history of conflict over doctrine and authority, exacerbated by the violent behavior in eastern Europe of the Western crusaders, resulted in the Eastern Schism (sometimes also called the Great Schism or East–West Schism) between the Eastern and Western Christian churches in 1054. (More on that later.) This split resulted in the Eastern Orthodox Church and the Roman Catholic Church. Finally, to stem doctrinal questions and perceived error, the Catholic Church instituted the Inquisition (a church tribunal that investigated matters of faith and doctrine), known for its often brutal treatment of alleged heretics (including Jews, Muslims, and persons considered witches).

Renaissance (Late Middle Ages)

This highly transitional period represents the apex of Roman Catholic political power. Key members of the hierarchical Catholic Church power structure came from noble families or were wealthy merchants who had risen to high social status. Remarkable building projects and artistic works inspired by classical Greek and Roman sculpture and architecture were commissioned by the popes themselves (and today constitute some of the most valuable treasures held by the Roman Catholic Church). Scholars and theologians produced some of the finest works of theology extant, still consulted as authoritative.

This era also saw the rise of independent, secular schools as centers for learning. Theology in these universities took on a new, speculative character, resulting in fresh debates and heresies. Political and theological conflicts arose in the Roman Catholic Church in the fourteenth century. Some conflicts stemmed from an increase in financial abuse by the popes and upper clergy. As successive popes demanded more and more financial support from the clergy, the clergy turned to the impoverished laity for money. The popes also experienced a great power struggle with French kings, compounded by the fact that from 1309 to 1377, seven popes resided in Avignon, France, instead of Rome, Italy. When the last of these popes, Gregory XI, left France and returned to Rome, some of the French cardinals were disgruntled. These same cardinals, feeling ill-treated under Gregory's successor, actually elected a second pope to rule from Avignon!

Although this period produced a multidimensional cultural "rebirth" (from which the term *Renaissance* comes), it also brought a time of corruption and excess that proved unsustainable in the following era.

The Reformation

Reformation is the general term used to describe the broad changes in Western Christian church doctrine, practice, and organized leadership that occurred from 1500 to 1750. Sometimes this period is called the Protestant Reformation, a name derived from the "protest" movement of German princes and cities against the edict of the Second Diet of Speyer (1529). This assembly of political and church leaders convened in Speyer, Germany, in 1529 and repealed the rulings of the First Diet of Speyer, in 1526. The original ruling had permitted freedom for religious reform, but in 1529 the Ottoman Turks were advancing on the lands of the Holy Roman Empire (HRE). To try to retain tax money for a united defense of the HRE, the new ruling prohibited religious reform and required obedience to the Catholic faith. As reformers protested this ruling, they began to be known as "Protestants."

Why was reform of the Roman Catholic Church necessary? To begin, as popes and kings had vied for power over the preceding centuries, the political situation of the Roman Catholic Church finally reached a breaking point during the Renaissance. Monarchs felt increasing anger and resentment when they found themselves politically subservient to and overtaxed by the Roman Catholic Church. These realities were compounded by a growing sense of nationalism among the city-states of Europe, especially among the peasantry, who saw the monetary comforts of the church and its clergy while they were left wanting. In addition, many European monarchs had made arrangements with the pope in which they retained immediate governance of their local churches. Such monarchs began to wonder whether they had any need for papal administration or affiliation.

The Roman Catholic Church also became corrupt in many ways during the Renaissance. Among the problems reformers noted were the selling of indulgences (or a remission of punishments for sin), exploitation of the poor, burdensome pilgrimage requirements, excessive veneration of saints, poor training and moral laxity among the clergy, and the vast financial wealth and landholdings of the church. These problems raised questions about the character and authority of the Bishop of Rome and the hierarchy under his administration. The question of authority was intensified by the fifteenth-century event known as the Western Schism (also called the Papal Schism), in which confusion arose over who of three contenders was the rightful pope following the period of the Avignon papacy.

Another cause underlying the Reformation was humanism. Largely spread by Erasmus of Rotterdam (1469–1536), humanism was an intellectual movement that stressed a return to classical sources. For theology, this meant a return to the patristic literature and, most importantly, to the Bible. Unlike the highly ordered scholastic theology of the previous era, the humanist movement encouraged speculative philosophy and freedom of inquiry, which flourished in the newly founded secular universities. Humanism also encouraged literacy among the general populace. This, coupled with new translations of the Bible in the vernacular (or common language) of the people, gave the average person immediate access to Scripture for the first time in Christian history. This trend was furthered by the advent of mass printing technology, which allowed for rapid, cheap reproduction of texts, pamphlets, and images. All of these factors combined to create a more learned and hence more critically aware citizenry, for whom an authoritative knowledge handed down from "on high" was replaced with study and discernment from the grassroots up.

The organizational and doctrinal reform of Christian churches during the Reformation varied greatly. For the purposes of classification, however, several major dimensions of the Reformation are usually noted. These include the following:

- Mainstream Reformation refers to the Lutheran and Reformed church movements. The Lutheran Reformation resulted from the efforts of German-born Martin Luther (1483–1546), whose critiques of Roman Catholic doctrine and practice resulted in a break from Roman authority and the institutionalization of a new church. Luther is often credited with starting the Reformation. The Reformed Church is the outgrowth of John Calvin's (1509–1564) second-generation reform efforts. Calvin was a Swiss-born theologian whose systematic approach to theology helped to order and institutionalize Protestant Christian doctrine.

- Radical Reformation refers to the reform efforts of a variety of sectarian groups, characterized by their rejection of many mainstream Christian practices. These groups, known variously as the Anabaptists and the "left wing of the Reformation," brought strong critiques to the institutional churches. Their sense of Christian community derived from close readings of the New Testament, and they sought to re-create the New Testament model in the sixteenth century. Notably, these groups stressed adult baptism (hence, rebaptism or anabaptism of those who were baptized as infants), common ownership of property, and pacifism.

- Catholic Reformation, also called the Counter-Reformation, was a movement within the Roman Catholic Church that tried to respond to the criticisms of the Protestant reformers. In this movement, the Catholic Church focused on founding service-oriented religious orders (such as the Ursulines and the Jesuits), cultivating spiritual discipline, educating the clergy, and morally improving the Roman Catholic Church leadership. The most significant move of the Catholic Reformation was the convening of the Council of Trent in 1545, in which the moral, doctrinal, and institutional developments of the Protestants were formally discussed, addressed, and denounced. In addition, the decrees of Trent introduced necessary reforms in the moral, spiritual, clerical, and service dimensions of Roman Catholicism. Through these reforms, many of the Protestants' grievances were corrected. Nevertheless, the theological and institutional differences between most Protestants and Catholics remained too deep to restore.

The Modern Era

The modern period of Christian history dates loosely from the mid-eighteenth century to the present day. Although any number of philosophical, technological, political, or social developments can be discussed as essential to this era, no specific selection could be exhaustive or sufficiently comprehensive. The modern period of Christianity has occurred in a global context during a time of scientific, cultural, and technological advancement unprecedented in human history. Perhaps the best way to consider the modern period of Christian thought is to simply note the breadth of topics one encounters in its study.

From the eighteenth century on, philosophical movements such as rationalism, empiricism, and the Enlightenment prevailed throughout Western Europe, England, and colonial North America. These movements placed great confidence in human reason, and by reason people sought to know the world, without the aid of religious faith, myth, or superstitions from the past. The effect was a shifting of truth from the purview of learned authorities or church teaching to the domain of the free human mind. Key Christian beliefs, for example, in the miracles of Christ or his Resurrection, were thus profoundly challenged in this "Age of Reason" and have remained matters of debate and reflection. Exemplary of this type of critique of Christian belief is Immanuel Kant's work, *Religion within the Limits of Reason Alone* (1793).

Church authority also shifted dramatically in the modern era. After the Reformation, the Roman Catholic Church did not regain the monolithic religious authority it had formerly enjoyed in the West. Nor did Protestant ecclesial institutions attain the unchallenged power that the Catholic Church wielded at its apex. Especially in colonial North America, church authority was largely relativized by the spirit of independence and reason-based inquiry. This change in authority over time has been enhanced further by a freer academic culture in both secular and church-affiliated universities. Although church authorities have often been reluctant to cede power, contemporary Christian people are today more likely to be instructed in matters of faith and practice than they are to be coerced or bound by legal or policy structures informed by church authorities. For example, the document *Ex Corde Ecclesiae* (From the Heart of the Church), promulgated by Pope John Paul II in 1990, which describes the identity and mission of Catholic colleges and universities and provides norms to help fulfill its vision, reveals the more dialogical nature of the relationship between Roman Catholic Church authority and Catholic colleges that is characteristic of the contemporary era.

After the Reformation, religious wars raged throughout Europe in the sixteenth and seventeenth centuries. Following decades of relentless bloodshed, a spirit of tentative religious tolerance and denominationalism (multiple Christian groups coexisting and going by different names) arose by default. The plethora of Christian groups throughout the world today has its origin in this era. At present, international organizations, such as the World Council of Churches (WCC), boast membership of hundreds of different Christian communions attempting both to resolve conflicts with one another and also to collaborate in practical ways for justice-oriented and peacemaking initiatives.

Democratic revolutions, such as the American and French Revolutions, occurred throughout Europe and America in the eighteenth and nineteenth centuries. Where monarchs once reigned, supported by the church establishment, new civil governments and laws emerged, based on Enlightenment principles that elevated the individual and cultivated a sense of common humanity. In Europe and America, religious faith was now largely removed from the formal statutes of the civil government in the classic "separation of church and state" model. An excellent example of this is the First Amendment to the Constitution of the United States of America, which states explicitly that the U.S. government can neither institute religion nor prohibit its free expression.

More recently, in the nineteenth century, Western culture underwent radical transformations. Among the most significant developments were industrialization, capitalism, Marxism, and the birth of modern science (spurred by Darwin's evolutionary theory). In the twentieth and twenty-first centuries, one observes unprecedented advances in travel, communication (including the personal computer, the Internet, and social networking), and warfare technology (including nuclear and biological warfare). Contemporary Christian culture is marked by dialogue with ongoing advances in medical technologies, social revolutions such as feminism and the gay rights movement, new forms of media and communication, the intellectual culture of postmodernism, and the turn to environmentalism and conservationism as broad social concerns.

In the twenty-first century, Christianity is present throughout most of the known world and continues to grow. There are thousands of Christian denominations, into which fall roughly two billion faithful followers worldwide. Moreover, Christianity is but one of many world religions, and a context of religious pluralism is assumed. Christians are represented across the range of academic fields of study, political parties, lifestyles, and professions. For its subscribers, Christian faith directs one's moral behavior in matters ranging from the use of medical technology, participation in war, and development of educational curricula to those as seemingly inconsequential as which (if any) TV programs to watch, companies to invest in, and fashions to wear. Christian thought is as varied as its adherents, and many Christian theologians argue that respecting diverse opinions among Christians is a foremost ethical and methodological concern in their work. Surveys of contemporary Christian thought, such as David Ford's helpful anthology *The Modern Theologians*, quickly reveal the diverse range of modern Christian belief and practice. Topics considered in Ford's anthology include the following:

- major contemporary theologians from the twentieth and twenty-first centuries
- theology in dialogue with the physical, biological, and social sciences
- theology in spiritual practice and pastoral application
- feminism and gender in theology
- black, Latin American, Hispanic, African, and Asian Christian theologies
- inter- and intrareligious dialogue
- Christian theology in dialogue with non-Christian religions
- theology in dialogue with politics
- theology in dialogue with visual arts, film, and music

In short, one can assume little about the contemporary Christian. Any study of Christian thought today should begin with a discussion of context: social and geographical location. Because there are hundreds of Christian church institutions, many of which have structures of organization at the international level, it may be more appropriate today to speak of "Christianities" rather than of Christianity.

Conclusion

Christian thought has grown and developed for two thousand years and cannot be understood outside its historical contexts. Christian thought in second-century Antioch differed widely from Christian thought in third-century Alexandria. Thought from both periods differs widely from Christian thought in sixth-century France, and so on. Today, Christian thought can differ tremendously from the church on the corner to the one down the street on any given Sunday. When studying Christian thought, one must attend to historical and contextual questions to arrive at a responsible and informed grasp of the issues. By exploring key questions, the rationale behind Christian theology and the formal expressions of faith and worship become clear. Some questions to consider asking when doing theology include the following:

- What is the era?
- What is the geographical location?
- What is the political situation?
- What is the status or quality of life for the average person?
- To what technologies, including medicine, do people have access?
- What is the average level of education?
- How could the economy of the era be described?
- What challenges, issues, or conflicts do people face?

Questions for Discussion and Review

1. What are the two major divisions in the biblical era?
2. Describe key aspects of the historical context of the Israelites in the Old Testament.
3. Describe five major challenges that the Christian community faced in the New Testament era.
4. Describe the patristic era and the reasons why development of doctrine was often a contentious process.

5. Name the time periods within the Middle Ages.

6. Give several reasons why the Reformation occurred. What are the major groupings of Reformation activity?

7. In your opinion, what are the three most influential cultural developments of the modern era that affect Christian thought? What challenges do you think Christian thinkers must face today?

8. What sorts of questions should one ask when considering Christian thought from a historical point of view?

Key Terms

Alexandria
Anabaptism
Antioch
apologia
Augustine
Babylonian Exile
Cappadocian fathers
Carthage
Catholic
  Reformation
Charlemagne
Clement of
  Alexandria

Constantine
Council of Nicaea
Cyrus the Great
Dark Ages
denominationalism
Eastern Schism
  (Great Schism)
Enlightenment
Exodus
humanism
intertestamental
Judas Maccabeus
Judges

Mainstream
  Reformation
modern era
Origen
patristic era
Renaissance
scholastic
Tertullian
vernacular
Western Schism
  (Papal Schism)

Resources

Baker, Robert A., and John M. Landers. *A Summary of Christian History*. 3rd ed. Nashville: Broadman and Holman, 2005.

Gonzalez, Justo. *Church History: An Essential Guide*. Nashville: Abingdon, 1996.

Jones, Timothy Paul. *Christian History Made Easy: 13 Weeks to a Better Understanding of Church History.* Torrance, CA: Rose, 1999, 2005.

McGrath, Alister E. *Historical Theology: An Introduction to the History of Christian Thought.* Oxford, UK: Blackwell, 1998.

Shelley, Bruce L. *Church History in Plain Language.* 3rd ed. Nashville: Thomas Nelson, 2008.

4 Christian Doctrines

What Is Doctrine?

As with any faith tradition, Christianity has numerous beliefs that characterize its worldview, or system of beliefs. Some of these beliefs are termed *doctrines*, deriving from the Latin word *docere*, meaning "to teach." There are many distinct Christian communities (which will be considered in the next chapter), each holding a different set of beliefs and practices. Some of their doctrinal differences are theologically significant, while others may be considered relatively minor. For example, some Christian groups baptize only adults or children of rational age, while others baptize infants as well as people of other ages. Some Christian groups, such as Seventh-Day Adventists and Seventh Day Baptists, worship on Saturday, because of the Old Testament commandment to observe the Sabbath. Most Christians, however, worship on Sunday because of the belief that Jesus' Resurrection was on Sunday. Some Christian groups ordain women, while others do not. These and other differences in practice are tied to the theological beliefs and rationales held by each of the church communities.

Throughout history, Christians have debated, and sometimes fought fiercely over, proper definitions of correct beliefs and practice. Even today, Christians still debate differences in belief, and some differences continue to be divisive (for example, attitudes regarding sexual lifestyle and leadership opportunities for homosexual persons in Christian churches). The degree to which differences are considered major or minor is determined largely by the groups themselves, because it is they who ascribe levels of importance to the distinctive aspects of their communities.

Despite differences in beliefs, Christians generally hold numerous key doctrines to be true (even if each group would explain these doctrines differently). Most Christian groups also have statements of faith, called creeds or confessions, that articulate their specific doctrines. (See also the section Creeds: Comparison of Statements of Faith, at the end of this chapter.)

Like the systems of a physical body, Christian doctrines work together, forming a holistic worldview. When well explicated, doctrines ideally have an internal logic or rationale, so that each doctrine complements the others, and together these doctrines form a reasonable whole, providing a persuasive account of human experience, the created world, and the ultimate destiny of all things. The integrative study of Christian doctrine is called systematic theology.

Because every doctrinal aspect of systematic theology is linked with the others, there is an overlapping quality to the study of an individual doctrine. For example, study of the doctrine of God overlaps the study of Jesus and the study of revelation. Deciding where to begin a discussion of individual Christian doctrines is somewhat arbitrary. Classic approaches to systematic theology often follow the sequence of God, Jesus, Holy Spirit, and church. This approach is derived from the Nicene Creed, which uses this pattern. The approach taken here generally follows this classic model.

God

A Christian conception of God begins with the models of God presented in the Bible. The biblical presentation of God is often analogical, meaning that it invokes various images and experiences drawn from ordinary life to suggest what God may be like. Images used throughout both the Old and New Testaments, such as Lord and King, reflect how the ancient, popular human imagination envisioned a powerful God. These images often inform how people think of God even today. Depictions of God as an elderly but powerful male sitting on a throne in the sky (think of such diverse examples as Michelangelo's depiction of God giving life to Adam on the Sistine Ceiling and Morgan Freeman's portrayal of God in the film *Bruce Almighty*) have their root in this biblical imagery. This imagery was particularly effective in the patriarchal context of the Bible's origin, in which lords and kings constituted the highest power among human beings.

Note, however, that well-known images such as these are not the only ones presented in the Bible. Other images, such as the mother hen (see Matthew 23:37 and Luke 13:34), the romantic lover (see the Song of Solomon), the Lady Wisdom (see Proverbs), or the beloved spouse (see Hosea) are also present. These lesser-known analogies for God help to deconcretize, or break down, the idea that God is actually a man who behaves like a king or a warlord.

Why are analogies used? The Christian tradition holds that God is simultaneously knowable and unknowable to the human mind because the human mind is itself limited. Even what we know by close observation, study, and reflection is subject to revision once more information is obtained or better tools for observation are available. Some aspects of human experience elude our comprehension altogether. As such, one must acknowledge the finite character of what human beings can know about the world.

By contrast, the Christian faith holds that God is infinite. Thus God has no limits. That which is limited (i.e., people) cannot fully grasp that which is limitless (i.e., God). Furthermore, people have only a limited experience with which to grasp the limitless foundation of experience. So all pronouncements about God must retain a tentative, metaphorical, or analogical character.

In Christian history, the biblical images of God were and continue to be processed through intellectual tradition. In the first centuries of the Christian era (30–600), this processing was informed largely by the methods and insights of Greek philosophy. The interface between philosophical and biblical thoughts regarding divinity resulted in several concepts that helped describe how Christians typically understand God. Though not exhaustive, key terms used to describe these concepts for understanding God include the following:

Personal. Christianity holds that God has a personal relationship with humanity and all other life. God is understood to be deeply relational and involved in the life of the world. As such, the Bible describes God as a parent, lover, spouse, and protector. Sometimes, it even depicts God as angry with, jealous over, or suffering on account of human life, all of which suggest a God who cares personally rather than a God who remains aloof or removed from the concerns of the world. A key indicator of the Christian conception of God as personal is the prayer tradition in Christian spirituality, which holds that God's action can be informed and even directed by the needs, wishes, and hopes of human beings.

Free. Christianity holds that God is free. This means God may choose to act or not to act. God could have chosen not to create, just as God chose to create. By claiming that God is free, Christians suggest that divine life is *agential* rather than merely process or necessity. This means that God is not uncontrollable power, like a spewing volcano, but rather a personal will that acts—by analogy—as a person acts when choosing to do something. God's freedom and God's personal character are thus intertwined in the Christian model.

All-Powerful. Christians understand God as all-powerful, or omnipotent. Thus God is the foremost cause of the universe. Christians further refine the concept of omnipotence by saying that God can even limit God's own power. An example of such self-limitation would be the laws of nature, which most Christians argue were established by God in creation and which, once established, remain fixed even beyond God's power to contravene. Christians believe that God limits divine power so that creation can be free rather than robotic. If God interfered in natural life, even for a good reason (such as to prevent an act of violence or suffering), the parties involved would have their essential freedom revoked. God's choice to limit God's power becomes actually the finest and fullest expression of God's might. Thus the notions of omnipotence and self-limit are twin aspects of the Christian conception of divine power.

All-Knowing. Related to God's omnipotence is the idea that God is all-knowing, or omniscient. This refers to the belief that God has full knowledge of all that was, is, could have been, and is yet to be. Although this aspect is debated, Christians typically do not believe that God's foreknowledge of events and human choices violates human freedom. Just as a person might be able to anticipate a car accident while looking on from a hilltop at out-of-control cars rushing toward one another, so some Christians have argued, God's ability to perceive an event does not compromise the freedom of the actors in the event. By extension, any pursuit in life might lead to illness, accident, mistake, or injury (driving a car, going to the beach, hiking through the woods, working as a doctor). If God were to stop people from doing such things because they might end poorly, God would ultimately stop life itself. By contrast, many Christians affirm God's providential love and total knowledge of creation, including human beings, from the moment of their inception to death, even while they affirm that God endows human beings with fundamental freedom to pursue life unhindered by divine interference.

Creator. Christians hold that God creates the universe. Although some people read the biblical description of creation in the book of Genesis as a literal account of creation, many Christians today affirm modern scientific understandings of cosmology and evolutionary theory as more accurate descriptions of natural history. Still, such Christians affirm that God is responsible for cosmological processes and evolution, as the providential power and free agent behind all natural events. This understanding of God as creator looks at biblical accounts as metaphoric truths about the origin of the universe. Such belief holds that the accounts do not tell us literally what happened but speak of the divine intention and power of creation.

Eternal. Christian faith holds that, just as God is infinite (or limitless), God has no beginning and no end.

One and Uniquely Divine. In Christian faith, God is the only being or substance in the universe that is self-sufficient. The being or substance of every other thing in the universe, and the universe itself, is derived from divine self-sufficiency. As such God is one (*mono*) and unique in the absolute qualities of eternality, limitlessness, power, knowledge, being-ness, freedom, and so on. No other divine powers—no other gods—but the one God exist.

Good. Christian faith holds that God is good. This goodness defines how Christians understand God's power. Even though God may have total power, God elects to act in a way that is good and loving, just and merciful, toward God's creation. Most Christians do not believe God acts arbitrarily or vindictively, or that God toys with people (as people believed the gods of the Greek and Roman pantheon did). Rather, Christian faith holds that God is the font of goodness and acts in ways that are essentially good and consistent with—although superior to—human conceptions of goodness.

Trinity

The terms previously considered characterize the general doctrine of God in Christian faith and are largely shared by Jewish and Islamic faiths. What distinguishes the Christian conception of God from that of these cousin faiths is the idea that God is tri-une, or Trinitarian. *Trinity* refers to the belief that God is three persons in one Godhead (which is the nature of God, especially as existing in three persons). These three persons are usually named Father, Son, and Holy Spirit. To move away from the exclusive use of male analogies, some contemporary Christians (borrowing from feminist writers such as Elizabeth Johnson and Sallie McFague) will also use other names to suggest the Trinitarian nature of God, such as: Creator, Redeemer, and Sustainer; or Mother, Lover, and Friend.

Skeptics might argue that the Trinity simply does not make sense. Three do not add up to one; one cannot be three. Christians, in fact, recognize the basic illogicality of the Trinitarian notion of God and thus often refer to the Trinity as a mystery that defies ultimate explanation and understanding.

How did Christians arrive at such a notion of God? To answer, it helps to consider that the doctrine of the Trinity sprang primarily from the belief in Jesus' divinity. In the early Christian period, followers of Jesus' way believed that Jesus was imbued with divine power and presence, but it remained unclear at first how Christians were to understand the nature of this power and presence. The use of different names in the New Testament to describe Jesus suggests that early Christians held an array of understandings of his identity. Such names include Messiah, Son of God, Son of Man, prophet. Each of these descriptions opened possible ways for thinking about Jesus in relationship to God. Was he a lesser god, a second god, a divine son (such as the Greek figures of Achilles and Hercules), or the one-and-only God come down from heaven?

As Christians tried to define their faith that Jesus was divine, they were at pains to preserve the oneness of God and the divinity (and later, the humanity) of Jesus. Over several centuries, Christian theologians developed key terms and ideas to try to explain how Jesus could be at once human and divine, as well as how Jesus could be divine without compromising the oneness of God. The following concepts help to explain the rationale of the Trinity.

Economy. This term derives from the Greek word *oikonomia*, which means "household management." Christian theologians argued that God's household was creation itself, and though God was distinct from creation, God nevertheless was involved in its affairs. The "economic" Trinity explained how God managed creation through different modes of action, such as creating, redeeming, and inspiring. The persons of the Trinity in this model were understood as expressing simultaneous yet distinctive aspects of God's interaction with the world. The Father refers to God's personal creative action, the Son refers to God's personal redemptive action in the life of Jesus, the Spirit to God's personal inspirational action.

Immanent. The economic Trinity is sometimes contrasted with the immanent Trinity, which refers to the inner logic of God's being. Early Christian theologians argued that a Trinitarian model was necessary for understanding God appropriately, because threeness expresses relationality within God's very self. For example, Richard of Saint Victor argued in the twelfth century that in a simple monotheism, one could argue that God is alone. In such isolation, God could be found wanting for companionship or love. For God to be deprived of these things would mean that God experienced a deficit and an imperfection, which they argued was inconsistent with the notion of an all-powerful and perfect God. In a Trinitarian model, by contrast, God is never alone but is internally relational. This type of argument builds upon that proffered by Augustine of Hippo in the fifth century, namely that the Trinity may be understood by the analogy of love, which requires three elements: a lover, a beloved, and the love between them.

Homoousios. This Greek term, which means "same substance," became a key element in explaining the Trinity. The term was incorporated in the creed produced by the Council of Nicaea in 325, which Christians continue to recite even today. In the face of great debate over the nature of the Trinity, the patristic-era Christians who prevailed at the Council of Nicaea argued that God's substance was distinct from the substance of everything else, because God alone in the universe is uncreated. Anything that had God's substance would therefore be God, while anything that did not have God's substance would be something created. In this way, the persons of the Trinity could be understood as distinct in their actions, as well as in their relationships to one another, and yet be one by virtue of their sharing the same divine substance.

Begetting/begotten/processing. As Christian theologians reflected further on the distinction of persons in the Trinity, they argued that the key element that made the persons distinct was their relationships to one another. The Father came to be understood as the one who eternally begets the Son. The Son came to be understood as the one who is eternally begotten of the Father. The Spirit came to be understood as the one who is eternally breathed (or processed) from the Father. Later, Western Christians added that the Spirit is eternally breathed by both the Father *and the Son* (the Latin term, *filioque*). The emphasis concerning all these relationships is twofold: (1) the relationships are eternal, and (2) the uniqueness of each person of the Trinity lies in the relational distinction and the action associated with that distinction vis-à-vis creation. The Father alone eternally begets the Son; the Son alone is eternally begotten; the Spirit alone eternally processes from the Father and the Son. Each person, furthermore, has distinct actions as Father, Son, or Spirit in the economy of salvation (see the discussion of "economic Trinity" above).

Because the Trinity remains a complex notion that is difficult to express, Christian councils identified two categorically flawed ways of understanding the Trinity. These included (1) any approach in which the distinctions between Father, Son, and Spirit are diminished so as to suggest that there is really only one person (for example, I am a single, individual person who sometimes acts as a teacher, other times as a mother, and other times as a writer), and (2) any approach in which the distinctions are so sharply contrasted as to create three separate deities.

JESUS IS *WHAT?*

The doctrine of God as Trinity and the doctrine of Christ as God are inseparable in Christian theology. The history of the evolution of thought on these foremost doctrines of Christian faith is fascinating. Because belief in Jesus is the core of Christianity, one might assume that Christians had a clear theological understanding of him from the beginning. The history of debates and councils from the second through the seventh centuries, however, tells a different story.

Driving one of the most important elements of debate was the question, Was Jesus fully human? The issue here was that if Jesus was fully human, then he could represent humanity in his sacrifice on the cross, expunging humanity's sin. If he was not fully human (like an angel or a demigod like Achilles), his sacrifice would not effect any change in humanity's fallen state (because it would be effective only for other angels or demigods or the like). Thus Jesus needs to be human in order to save. However, if Jesus was fully human, then how could he be divine at the same time?

Continued

Continued

Popular solutions in the second century were offered by such groups as the Docetists and the Gnostics. They argued, respectively, that Jesus only appeared to be human and that his humanity was irrelevant to humanity's salvation. By the beginning of the third century, groups such as the Ebionites emerged, who argued that Jesus was fully human and was only the "adopted" son of God (not God eternally but only becoming so after some point in Jesus' human life). By the fourth century, the question of Jesus' humanity came to a head because of the beliefs of a group known as the Arians. This group held that Jesus was the greatest of all creatures (not begotten of God as a son but made by God as other creatures are made). The debate was so fierce that the new Christian emperor, Constantine, summoned the bishops to Nicaea in 325 to settle the issue. The dominant position was that the Second Person of the Trinity, incarnate in Jesus, was "eternally begotten of the Father, God from God, Light from Light, true God from true God, begotten, not made, one in Being with the Father."

Even though the Council of Nicaea produced a creed that established the relationship between the Father and the Son, it did not settle all questions. For example, in the fourth and fifth centuries, the questions arose as to whether Jesus had a human soul as other humans have souls, whether Jesus was really two persons (one human and one divine) existing in one human body, and whether Mary could be called the Mother of God or was just the mother of the human aspect of Jesus. In the seventh century, the question arose again in a slightly different way: Did Jesus have a human will only, a divine will only, or both? Councils met throughout the fourth through the seventh centuries to resolve these questions.

Analogies. To help explain the possibility of three-in-one, Christian theologians have compared the Trinity to a number of ordinary objects experienced in daily life. Some examples include a triangle; a three-leafed clover; the water that flows in a spring, river, and sea; and a tree that has roots, branches, and leaves.

Revelation

Even with the help of the previous terms, the Christian conception of God as Trinitarian would not be possible apart from the claim that God has revealed this information about himself. Christian faith holds that though God can be known partially through study of the natural world, God makes full self-disclosure through self-revelation. Through that self-revelation, God tells people what God is like. A parallel in everyday life occurs when people reveal information about themselves to other people that would otherwise be unknowable to those people, like telling a friend about a recurring dream.

There are different ways of thinking about revelation, and not all Christians agree on what constitutes revelation or how it should be understood. Although not an exhaustive list of ways to think about revelation, three important modes will be considered here: revelation in scripture, revelation in history, and revelation in doctrine.

Revelation in scripture refers to the idea that the foremost place where God is revealed is in the sacred literature of the Bible. Revelation began with ancient Israel. God reveals his law and wisdom through the history and writings of the Israelites as recorded in the Old Testament. This revelation continues in the writings of the New Testament, which present the story of Jesus' life and its meaning for the first Christian communities. In the New Testament, revelation occurs in layers. On one layer, Jesus' teachings reveal truth about the nature of God and God's desires for humanity. On another, Jesus himself is the message of that revelation, meaning that the content of God's revelation is Jesus disclosing himself as God to humanity. On yet another layer, the text of the New Testament itself becomes an ongoing source of revelation for Christians who read, teach, and preach on the basis of its contents. (The final book of the New Testament is called the book of Revelation, but revelation in the New Testament includes all twenty-seven of its books.) Most Christians affirm the Bible as the foremost location of God's revelation.

Revelation in history refers to the idea that history itself is a place where God is self-revealing through God's action. By virtue of God's role in creating and sustaining the world, indeed the universe, the whole cosmic history reveals something of God's character, presence, and will. In this model, the Bible is revelation because it bears witness to and attempts to interpret God's action in the history of Israel and specifically in the life of Jesus. As an example of how this might happen in ordinary experience, imagine a person surviving a major natural disaster. In the wake of that experience, she has a new sense of purpose and meaning and dedicates her life to relief efforts for other survivors. When asked why she works as she does, she reports that it is because God acted in her life, and through that action has invited her to be an agent for helping others. This woman is seeing God's will revealed directly in the historical events of her life and continuing that revelation through her service to others. Revelation in history may be extended to include the notion that revelation occurs in the natural world and may be known through chemistry, biology, physics, and the other sciences.

Revelation in doctrine refers to the idea that direct revelation of God in history, captured in the biblical record, can be further communicated in Christian doctrine. Many elements of Christian faith are rooted in the Bible but are not presented there in a clear and teachable manner. One such example is the doctrine of the Trinity. Although biblical language discusses God as Father, God as Son, and God as Spirit, there is no articulation in the Bible that these are three persons in one God, that they share the same substance, or that by that shared substance they are coequal and coeternal. Christian theologians formulated this doctrine on the basis of the Bible, but in language that extended beyond the Bible. Christian doctrine, when developed and preserved by the official structures of Christian churches, is often considered by those churches to be an extension of God's biblical and historical revelation.

Jesus the Christ

Although God's revelation in Israel's history precedes Jesus both chronologically and contextually, the key element of revelation, from which all other Christian teaching flows, is Jesus himself. Jesus is the central figure of the Christian faith, so it is important to know something of his historical life, as well as how he is perceived in the Christian faith.

Jesus was a Jewish man who lived from roughly 4 BCE to 30 CE and whose life and teaching form the basis of the Christian faith. Although few people debate the historical existence of Jesus, little is known of his human life. What is known is drawn primarily from the four Gospels in the Bible: Matthew, Mark, Luke, and John.

Details about Jesus' life that many scholars typically hold as true include the following: Jesus lived in northern Palestine near the Sea of Galilee, where much of his ministry took place. He was likely a skilled tradesman who worked as a carpenter or stonemason. Details in the Gospels suggest that his family observed Jewish laws and customs, such as traveling to Jerusalem for feast days. In his late twenties, Jesus was baptized by John the Baptist, after which he began a short career as an itinerant preacher. His preaching and teaching took the form of parables (short stories with an unexpected moral lesson), proverbial sayings (brief tokens of wisdom), and prophetic actions (such as healing on the Sabbath even though it was against Jewish laws or dining with "unclean" people even though it was a social taboo to do so). His ministry was oriented largely toward people pushed to the margins of society (such as those with contagious diseases or "unclean" professions or those usually considered sinners). The basic content of his message was the advent of the "kingdom of God" or the "kingdom of heaven," for which people needed to prepare by means of repentance from their sinful lives.

Jesus was a charismatic figure with a powerful ability to persuade. He gained a reputation as a healer and an exorcist and drew large crowds as he preached and traveled. He had a close coterie of disciples who traveled with him and were responsible for sharing his message after his death. Scholars debate whether Jesus saw himself as the Son of God, or merely as a prophet. What is clear, however, is that local religious and Roman political authorities perceived Jesus as a threat to the standing social order because he challenged their teaching and particularly their treatment of "undesirable" people. This challenge, for example, was manifest in Jesus' violent disruption of commercial activity in the Temple, where people were buying animals for religious sacrifices. While turning over the money-changers' tables, Jesus said that the house of God should not be a location for commerce (see Matthew 21:12, Mark 11:15, Luke 19:45, and John 2:15). As a result, during his visit to Jerusalem for the Passover feast, he was charged with political insurrection, arrested, tried, humiliated, and executed. His manner of death was crucifixion, which was death by suffocation while nailed to a cross and physically exposed to the elements. Although the Jewish high court was responsible for Jesus' arrest, his death fell under the jurisdiction of the Roman governor, Pontius Pilate. (Accounts of Jesus' arrest, trial, and execution begin in Matthew 26:47, Mark 14:43, Luke 22:47, and John 18). After his death, Jesus was buried in the tomb of Joseph of Arimathea. At the time of Jesus' death, the Bible stories record that Jesus' friends denied their relationship with him and fled from his side, perhaps from fear that they too would be executed.

Although the sketch just rendered covers generally accepted details of Jesus' human life, the Christian religion is based largely on claims about Jesus that are made and accepted through faith. For this reason, many scholars differentiate between the Jesus of history and the Jesus of faith. Faith-based claims about the life and significance of Jesus began three days after his death, when some of Jesus' female companions visited his tomb and found it empty (the Gospel accounts vary as to which women visited the tomb). The Bible records that this event was a visitation, whereby an angel told the women not to look for Jesus in his tomb. The account in the Gospel of Matthew 28:1–10 reads as follows:

> After the Sabbath, as the first day of the week was dawning, Mary Magdalene and the other Mary came to see the tomb. And behold there was a great earthquake; for an angel of the Lord descended from heaven, approached, rolled back the stone, and sat upon it. His appearance was like lightning and his clothing was white as snow. The guards were shaken with fear of him and became like dead men. Then the angel said to the women in reply, "Do not be afraid! I know that you are seeking Jesus the crucified. He is not here, for he has been raised just as he said. Come and see the place where he lay. Then go quickly and tell his disciples, 'He has been raised from the dead, and he is going before you to Galilee;

there you will see him.' Behold, I have told you." Then they went away quickly from the tomb, fearful yet overjoyed, and ran to announce this to his disciples. And behold, Jesus met them on their way and greeted them. They approached, embraced his feet, and did him homage. Then Jesus said to them, "Do not be afraid. Go tell my brothers to go to Galilee, and there they will see me."

The Christian pronouncement that Jesus is risen from the dead is known as the Resurrection. Also called the Easter event, the Resurrection led to the claim by Jesus' friends, and later by many converts, both pagan and Jewish, that he was the Messiah of ancestral hope. Jesus was also identified as the *Christ*, the Greek equivalent of the Hebrew word *Messiah*, both of which mean "anointed one."

The first phase of the Christian movement, roughly 30–110 CE, commenced with the teaching that Jesus was resurrected and that his followers could also hope for resurrection after death if they lived according to Jesus' teaching and in communion with other Christian people. Jesus had revealed the nature of the kingdom of God, the purpose of human life, and the moral conduct expected of people covenanted to God. By Jesus' revelation of the kingdom of God, people could be saved from both the disappointments of life and the finality of death.

As followers of this new movement began to reflect on their belief that Jesus was the long hoped-for Messiah, the savior, they asked questions about his exact nature. Other great prophets had lived and taught a moral way of life before Jesus, but they nevertheless had not been considered saviors. Christians reasoned that Jesus was indeed a human being. He had lived a fully human life, filled with friendships, sorrow, temptations, hope, fear, and finally death. Yet a human being alone could not accomplish the miracles he performed, nor could a human being of his own power rise from the dead. Thus Christians further concluded that Jesus was also divine. Christian theologians debated the question of his precise nature over the next several centuries (as we see in the discussion of Trinity above). Among the most significant aspects of Jesus' nature that theologians articulated are the following claims:

- Through Jesus' Incarnation in human life, death, and Resurrection, humanity is saved from sin and ultimately reconciled with God.

- Jesus is fully human and fully divine, having two distinct natures in one person. These natures are not confused or combined but are rather fully intact and copresent.

- Jesus had a fully human will and a fully divine will, distinct yet simultaneously present in one person.

- Jesus was the Incarnation of the Second Person of the Trinity, whose distinct action as the Son was to become incarnate (or enfleshed). The Father and the Spirit, thus, did not experience the human life or death on the cross as the Son did.

- Mary, Jesus' mother, conceived Jesus by the power of the Holy Spirit. He did not have a human, biological father. The person Jesus incarnated in Mary's body was fully divine and fully human at the time of his conception, and thus it is proper to refer to Mary as the Mother of God.

- Jesus really died, and Jesus really rose from the dead; in other words, his death was not an illusion or an appearance. Thus God understands and experiences death itself, even though God never properly died or temporarily went out of existence.

- Because Jesus was fully human and fully divine, as God Incarnate, he is humanity's savior.

- Jesus revealed that God is Trinitarian and not simply a monotheistic deity.

Salvation, Sin, and Grace

Driving the Christological (pertaining to the study of Christ) debates about Jesus' nature was the fundamental Christian belief that Jesus was the savior of the world. His short life and violent death would not have occasioned hope and a new religious movement apart from the belief that Jesus saved people in some elemental, essential way. Why did people feel the need to be saved, and how did they think Jesus' life and death provided that salvation? These questions lie at the heart of the theological task called soteriology (meaning "study of *soteria*"—the Greek word for "salvation"). To fully appreciate what the Christian concept of salvation means, one must understand two other Christian concepts related to the religious study of the human person. This study, properly termed *theological anthropology*, concerns the doctrines of sin and grace.

Sin is the name Christians ascribe to the fundamental brokenness or fallenness in the world. Based on the biblical account of the creation of human beings, Christians hold that humans were created with free will. This means that God intended people to be independent moral agents capable of making decisions about how they lived. The Bible indicates, however, that the first human beings abused their freedom by disobeying God. The wholesomeness of creaturely life was thus impaired. The sin of disobedience had at its root egotistical self-love, which may be found at the core of all other types of bad actions and vices, including greed, lust, wrath, gluttony, sloth, pride, and so on.

Sin is experienced as original in every human life as a result of our being born into a corporate (or collective) sinful condition at the societal level and as a matter of history. For example, if a parent exposes her children to prejudice or bad habits, her children will experience a sinful condition in the dysfunction of their homes in childhood, and they may also be inclined to reproduce those same behaviors as adults. Sin is also experienced as personal in the human life when individuals succumb to egotistical or selfish thoughts and deeds. On account of sin, both personal and corporate, humanity lost its paradisiacal existence and marred its friendship with God.

The broken relationship between humanity and God required repair. However, this repair was beyond humanity's power to effect on its own. God thus aided humanity by becoming incarnate in human life. Christianity understands Jesus as the one, by virtue of his joint human and divine natures, who would be able to repair this rift. As a human being, he was obliged to live in right relationship to God; as God himself, Jesus had the power to overcome human sin and selfishness so as to model and live out a proper human response to God. Through the excellence of his life and also his death, which was offered by Jesus as a free self-sacrifice, human beings gained an advocate and a mediator in the Trinity. Christians believe that after his Resurrection, Jesus ascended to heaven, taking his humanity with him, and now helps human beings through the gift of grace.

Christians believe grace is the special way Jesus extends his unmerited friendship and forgiveness to sinful humanity. Different Christian groups debate how Jesus' grace saves or affects people. Indeed, some of the fiercest historical debates in Christianity center on the question of how Jesus' grace operates in and for human life. A common, though not exclusive, way that Christians explain grace involves Jesus' death. The belief is that Jesus' death atoned for (or made up for) the disordered relationship between God and humanity that resulted from sin. Once sin was repaired, humans could experience deliverance from the consequences of sin (namely, suffering and death) if they followed Christ. Christ gives grace to his followers, who are thereby justified (or sanctified or made righteous) and ultimately saved to eternal life with the risen Christ. Different ways Christians have understood the operation of grace include the following:

- Grace is imparted internally to the person through the gift of faith, and by faith, people are saved. In this model, faith is like a seed planted in a person, which grows and blossoms throughout life.

- Grace covers a sinner as a cloak covers a body. The person remains internally sinful but is saved by the cover of Christ's righteousness. In this model, a person is inherently unchanged but nevertheless protected by Christ as a winter coat protects from the cold.

- Human beings are given grace internally in their willpower, and by this grace are able to cooperate with God in the performance of good deeds. In this understanding, people over time contribute positively toward their own salvation. An analogy for this model of grace might be an athlete who has been given a gift of speed or agility but has to use and cultivate that gift through practice to become excellent at her sport.

- The grace of Christ comes by way of the moral example he set in his life and death. In this model, people are so moved by Jesus' example as to become morally improved in their own lives. The slogan "What Would Jesus Do?" often seen on bracelets and bumper stickers, captures the essence of this understanding of grace.

Church and Sacraments

The role of the church in Christian doctrine is connected intimately with both the doctrine of Christ's Incarnation and the doctrine of grace. Christians believe that Jesus ascended to heaven forty days after his Resurrection. Upon Jesus' ascension, his physical, earthly presence was lost to humanity. The biblical story of Pentecost recounts that fifty days after the ascension, Jesus' disciples and followers experienced an outpouring of the Holy Spirit, after which time they understood that their task was to spread the good news about Jesus throughout the world. This event marks the beginning of the Christian church.

As ministers of this new church, Jesus' early followers believed themselves to be empowered by the Holy Spirit to continue Jesus' work in the world and for the redemption of all people. Composed of real human beings inspired by God's Spirit and made holy by Christ's grace, the church, as Christians came to understand it, was the ongoing, incarnational presence of God in the world.

Christians therefore have used physical and bodily metaphors for describing the nature of the church from its inception. Terms Christians frequently have used from the time of the New Testament until the present day to describe the church include *Body of Christ*, *People of God*, and *brothers and sisters in Christ*. Roman Catholic and Orthodox Christians extend bodily references to the church with the claim that during their sacramental worship services (to be discussed next), the ministers act in the person of Christ, and through them the bread and wine are transformed into the literal body and blood of Christ.

The study of the church is called ecclesiology, deriving its name from the Greek word *ekklesia*, meaning "congregation" or "assembly." Christian groups espouse a variety of ecclesiologies, so it is difficult to provide one inclusive sense of how Christians understand themselves as church. The differences among various Christian worship communions (religious groups within Christianity with their own sets of beliefs and practices, especially a Christian denomination) will be discussed in the following chapter. For now, it is sufficient to note that for all Christians, the idea of church represents a community of Christian people, as opposed to a building or even an institutional organization. As a community of believers, the church plays a vital role in the way individual Christians experience their faith. It is also critical to Christians' understanding of the way in which Jesus' grace is made available to them.

Many churches teach that the sacraments are the principle conveyor of grace to Christians. Sacraments are rites or practices in the worship life of the community that Christians believe communicate God's grace to them in a special or unique way. As actions of the church community, sacraments represent the special way that Christian salvation is thought to be communal rather than individualistic. Most Christian communities celebrate two sacraments: baptism and the Eucharist (also called the Last Supper, the Lord's Supper, and Holy Communion).

Baptism is a sacrament of initiation in which the person is immersed in water (or has water drizzled on the forehead), in the name of the Father, Son, and Holy Spirit. This act signifies the cleansing of sin and entrance into the community. Some groups baptize only adults, while others baptize infants and children (as well as adults) on the basis of the parents' intention to raise the child as a Christian. The Eucharist is the memorial celebration of the last meal Jesus had with his disciples, during which he instructed them to break bread and drink wine in memory of how his body and blood were broken and shed on their behalf. Some groups believe that through the ritual reenactment, Jesus' body and blood are really made present, while others believe the ritual is only a symbolic representation of the event.

Other sacraments that Christians (particularly Roman Catholic and Orthodox) may observe include confirmation, holy orders, matrimony, penance and reconciliation, and anointing of the sick. Confirmation is the sacrament of commissioning, in which a baptized Christian is anointed with oil and thereby specially graced to do God's work in the world. Holy orders is the sacrament whereby an individual is ordained into the priesthood. In the sacrament of matrimony, Christians recognize marriage to be a religious vocation and special occasion of grace. Reconciliation, also called penance, is the sacrament whereby a Christian confesses sin and through acts of contrition restores a proper relationship with God and the church. In the anointing of the sick (the sacrament of healing), holy oil is administered to one experiencing physical or psychological disease for the purpose of bringing peace and spiritual healing.

Although various Christian groups observe different sacramental practices, the practices' character as material acts or rites captures the incarnational theology that Christ's saving grace is made tangible, even physically present, to Christians through the life of the church. Thus sacraments connect powerfully to the bodily and physical images by which Christians understand God's presence in the world through the church.

Eschatology

This chapter has considered a range of central Christian doctrines, all of which fundamentally express a belief that Jesus brings salvation to his followers. The final hope of that salvation is that Christians will enjoy resurrected life with Jesus after their mortal lives end. Christians recognize that although they speak of salvation as if it is already occurring or in process, final or ultimate salvation is not yet realized. Christian faith, therefore, has an already-but-not-yet quality to it. This characteristic is properly identified by the term *eschatology*, which means "study of the last things."

All aspects and dimensions of Christian doctrine are somewhat eschatological, or oriented toward a future fullness. For example, the Christian church is in the process of becoming; it is at present imperfect and regularly subject to revision and correction. Salvation from sin, as another example, is in process in Christian lives but is not yet complete (otherwise, people would be perfect, which few would argue is the case). The world itself is in process. Though Christians hold that God originated the world and constantly creates and sustains it, the final destiny of the world is still to come. As such, Christians typically hope for a time in which the whole world, indeed the universe itself, will be perfected under the full reign of God's will and goodness. Christians often use the biblical language of a "kingdom of God" to express metaphorically the idea of everything being perfectly ordered under the benevolent rule of God.

Beyond the generally eschatological nature of all Christian doctrine, Christians have specific expectations or hopes for the future. Different Christian communities articulate these with sometimes great variety, depending on their unique characteristics as a church. Some of the eschatological doctrines that Christian groups commonly hold, with variations among groups, include the following:

- **The Second Coming of Christ.** The belief that the risen Christ will return to Earth to usher in the final days and events of this present world (also called the Parousia or the Advent). Elements variously believed to be associated with the Second Coming include the rapture, a time of tribulation, and a period of peace. Christians debate the anticipated order of events and time frame associated with Jesus' return.

- **Resurrection and judgment.** Beliefs that Christians will rise from death to face judgment about the moral quality of their lives. Many believe that the physical body will be restored at the time of resurrection, while others believe that each person will be given a "spiritual" body, the nature of which is presently unknowable.

- **Heaven.** The belief that under God's full reign, evil and suffering in every manifestation (including death) will be overcome. Some believe that all persons, indeed all creation, will be restored and perfected after the resurrection. Others believe that only Christians (called the "elect") will experience heaven. Still others believe that only particularly chosen Christians (the "elect within the elect"), will experience heaven. Heaven has frequently been imagined as a physical space, but it is also appropriate to conceive of heaven as a nonspatial state of being in oneness with God.

- **Hell.** The belief that persons who by their own free will ultimately refuse God's offer of salvation and friendship will not ascend to heaven but will experience afterlife removed from the being and presence of God. Because hell is conceived of as existence in the absence of God's goodness, it is understood to be a torturous existence. As with heaven, however, it is not necessary to think of hell as a physical space rife with fire and pain. Nor is it necessary to think of hell as eternal. Hell can also be conceived of as a shadowlike state of being in total isolation.

• **Purgatory.** The belief that persons who have lived a fine, but imperfect, life will experience a period of cleansing before realizing their final destiny in heaven. Some historical notions of purgatory imagine it as akin to a "waiting room," although contemporary conceptions liken it more to the experience of one's eyes adjusting to the brightness of the sun.

Conclusion

Christian doctrine may be viewed from any number of angles, and it is appropriate to discuss the full range of Christian thought from any doctrine considered. One could begin a systematic consideration of Christian thought with a discussion of brokenness in the human experience; one could also begin with creation or God as revealed in nature or Jesus himself. The aim of any treatment of Christian doctrine is to understand how the system of faith comprehensively accounts for human experience of the world in light of Christian revelation. This chapter has provided a basic introduction to essential Christian doctrines including God; Trinity; revelation; Jesus the Christ; salvation, sin, and grace; church and sacraments; and eschatology.

The caveat offered at the beginning of the chapter is reiterated at the end: doctrine cannot be overgeneralized. Each Christian communion takes the individual doctrines and systematizes them in its own way. This is not to suggest that there are no similarities, or that there are only vague similarities. There are great similarities. Still, one finds in the study of Christian doctrine sometimes profound differences in belief, nuances in how a doctrine is expressed or understood, worship structure, organizational patterns, recognition of authority, and use of the Bible. This chapter has provided a rudimentary architecture, with accompanying terminology, for thinking about Christian doctrine. More advanced study would take place within the context of a single Christian communion.

Questions for Discussion and Review

1. Describe your understanding of systematic theology.

2. Choose three Christian doctrines discussed in this chapter and describe how they systematically work together.

3. Why is Christian language about God necessarily metaphorical?

4. What terms help you understand the doctrine of the Trinity? How would you describe this doctrine to a child?

5. How do Christians understand Jesus as both God and human? How do both natures relate to the idea that Jesus is the savior?

6. Describe the three modes of revelation considered in this chapter. How do they relate to one another?

7. What is the relationship among salvation, sin, and grace in the Christian understanding of the human person?

8. How does the idea of church relate to the idea of grace?

9. Why are Christian doctrines all eschatological in some way?

Key Terms

agential	grace	omniscient
baptism	heaven	processing
begetting	hell	purgatory
begotten	*homoousios*	Resurrection
Christ	immanent	revelation
Christological	Incarnation	sacraments
Easter	Jesus of faith	Second Coming
ecclesiology	Jesus of history	sin
economy	Messiah	
eschatology	monotheistic	
Eucharist	omnipotence	

COMPARISON OF STATEMENTS OF FAITH

NICENE-CONSTANTINOPOLITAN CREED, 381

We believe in one God,
the Father, the Almighty,
maker of heaven and earth,
and of all that is, seen and unseen.

We believe in one Lord, Jesus Christ,
the only Son of God,
eternally begotten of the Father,
God from God, Light from Light,
true God from true God,
begotten, not made, one in Being with the Father.
Through him all things were made.
For us men and for our salvation,
he came down from heaven:
by the power of the Holy Spirit
he was born of the Virgin Mary, and became man.
For our sake he was crucified under Pontius Pilate;
he suffered, died, and was buried.
On the third day he rose again
in fulfillment of the Scriptures;
he ascended into heaven
and is seated at the right hand of the Father.
He will come again in glory to judge
the living and the dead,
and his kingdom will have no end.

We believe in the Holy Spirit,
the Lord, the giver of life,
who proceeds from the Father and the Son.
With the Father and the Son he
is worshipped and glorified.
He has spoken through the Prophets.

Continued

Continued

We believe in one holy catholic
and apostolic Church.
We acknowledge one baptism
for the forgiveness of sins.
We look for the resurrection of the dead,
and the life of the world to come.
Amen.

PRESBYTERIAN CHURCH, GENERAL ASSEMBLY MISSION COUNCIL'S "BRIEF STATEMENT OF FAITH," 1983

In life and in death we belong to God.
Through the grace of our Lord Jesus Christ,
the love of God,
and the communion of the Holy Spirit,
we trust in the one triune God, the Holy One of Israel,
whom alone we worship and serve.

We trust in Jesus Christ,
Fully human, fully God.
Jesus proclaimed the reign of God:
preaching good news to the poor
and release to the captives,
teaching by word and deed
and blessing the children,
healing the sick
and binding up the brokenhearted,
eating with outcasts,
forgiving sinners,
and calling all to repent and believe the gospel.
Unjustly condemned for blasphemy and sedition,
Jesus was crucified,
suffering the depths of human pain
and giving his life for the sins of the world.
God raised Jesus from the dead,
indicating his sinless life,

Continued

Continued

breaking the power of sin and evil,
delivering us from death to life eternal.

We trust in God,
whom Jesus called Abba, Father.
In sovereign love God created the world good
and makes everyone equally in God's image
male and female, of every race and people,
to live as one community.
But we rebel against God; we hide from our Creator.
Ignoring God's commandments,
we violate the image of God in others and ourselves,
accept lies as truth,
exploit neighbor and nature,
and threaten death to the planet entrusted to our care.
We deserve God's condemnation.
Yet God acts with justice and mercy to redeem creation.
In everlasting love,
the God of Abraham and Sarah chose a covenant people
to bless all families of the earth.
Hearing their cry,
God delivered the children of Israel
from the house of bondage.
Loving us still,
God makes us heirs with Christ of the covenant.
Like a mother who will not forsake her nursing child,
like a father who runs to welcome the prodigal home,
God is faithful still.

We trust in God the Holy Spirit,
everywhere the giver and renewer of life.
The Spirit justifies us by grace through faith,
sets us free to accept ourselves and to love God and neighbor,
and binds us together with all believers
in the one body of Christ, the Church.
The same Spirit

Continued

Continued

who inspired the prophets and apostles
rules our faith and life in Christ through Scripture,
engages us through the Word proclaimed,
claims us in the waters of baptism,
feeds us with the bread of life and the cup of salvation,
and calls women and men to all ministries of the church.
In a broken and fearful world
the Spirit gives us courage
to pray without ceasing,
to witness among all peoples to Christ as Lord and Savior,
to unmask idolatries in Church and culture,
to hear the voices of peoples long silenced,
and to work with others for justice, freedom, and peace.
In gratitude to God, empowered by the Spirit,
we strive to serve Christ in our daily tasks
and to live holy and joyful lives,
even as we watch for God's new heaven and new earth,
praying, "Come, Lord Jesus!"

With believers in every time and place,
we rejoice that nothing in life or in death
can separate us from the love of God in Christ Jesus our Lord.

Glory be to the Father, and to the Son, and to the Holy Spirit. Amen.

MENNONITE CHURCH GENERAL CONFERENCE "BRIEF STATEMENT OF FAITH," 1963

1. We believe in one God eternally existing as Father, Son, and Holy Spirit.
2. We believe that God has revealed himself in the Scriptures of the Old and New Testaments, the inspired Word of God, and supremely in his Son, the Lord Jesus Christ.
3. We believe that in the beginning God created all things by His Son. He made man in the divine image, with free will, moral character, and a spiritual nature.

Continued

Continued

4. We believe that man fell into sin, bringing depravity and death upon the race; that as sinner, man is self-centered and self-willed, unwilling and unable to break with sin.

5. We believe that there is one Mediator between God and men, the Man Christ Jesus, who died to redeem us from sin and arose for our justification.

6. We believe that salvation is by grace through faith in Christ, a free gift bestowed by God on those who repent and believe.

7. We believe that the Holy Spirit convicts of sin, effects the new birth, gives guidance in life, empowers for service, and enables perseverance in faith and holiness.

8. We believe that the church is the body of Christ, the brotherhood of the redeemed, a disciplined people obedient to the Word of God, and a fellowship of love, intercession, and healing.

9. We believe that Christ commissioned the church to go into all the world, making disciples of all the nations, and ministering to every human need.

10. We believe it is the will of God that there should be ministers to teach the Word, to serve as leaders, to administer the ordinances, to lead the church in the exercise of discipline, and to serve as pastors and teachers.

11. We believe that those who repent and believe should be baptized with water as a symbol of baptism with the Spirit, cleansing from sin, and commitment to Christ.

12. We believe that the church should observe the communion of the Lord's Supper as a symbol of his broken body and shed blood, and of the fellowship of his church, until his return.

13. We believe in the washing of the saints' feet as a symbol of brotherhood, cleansing, and service, and in giving the right hand of fellowship and the holy kiss as symbols of Christian love.

14. We believe that God has established unique roles for man and woman, symbolized by man's bared head in praying and prophesying, and by woman's veiled head.

Continued

Continued

15. We believe that Christian marriage is intended by God to be the union of one man and one woman for life, and that Christians shall marry only in the Lord.

16. We believe that Christians are not to be conformed to the world, but should seek to conform to Christ in every area of life.

17. We believe that Christians are to be open and transparent in life, ever speaking the truth, and employing no oaths.

18. We believe that it is the will of God for Christians to refrain from force and violence in human relations and to show Christian love to all men.

19. We believe that the state is ordained of God to maintain order in society, and that Christians should honor rulers, be subject to authorities, witness to the state, and pray for governments.

20. We believe that at death the unsaved enter into everlasting punishment and the saved into conscious bliss with Christ, who is coming again, and will raise the dead, sit in judgment, and bring in God's everlasting kingdom.

Resources

Bettenson, Henry, ed. *Documents of the Christian Church.* Oxford and New York: Oxford University Press, 1999.

Erickson, Millard J. *Introducing Christian Doctrine.* 2nd ed. Grand Rapids, MI: Baker Academic, 2001.

Fiorenza, Francis Schussler, and John C. Galvin, eds. *Systematic Theology: Roman Catholic Perspectives.* 2nd ed. Minneapolis: Fortress, 2011.

Gaurino, Thomas G. *Foundations of Systematic Theology.* New York: Clark International, 2005.

Johnson, Luke Timothy. *The Creed: What Christians Believe and Why It Matters.* New York: Doubleday, 2004.

Migliore, Daniel L. *Faith Seeking Understanding: An Introduction to Christian Theology.* 2nd ed. Grand Rapids, MI: Eerdmans, 2004.

5 | Diversity in Christian
CHAPTER | Worship Communities

WHAT TO EXPECT

This chapter is a basic introduction to the major divisions within Christian worship groups. It will discuss the following:

- early Christian diversity
- branches of Eastern Christianity
- Roman Catholic Christianity
- Protestant groups of the Reformation and beyond
- the ecumenical movement

What Is a Christian Communion?

Christianity is a broad term that encompasses a vast range of beliefs, practices, and historical epochs. Although Christianity began in first-century Palestine, it has spread and changed throughout the world for less than two thousand years. Even at its inception, Christianity was a diverse phenomenon.

The Gospels in the New Testament suggest the existence of a variety of communities that followed Christ, yet maintained slightly different interpretations of his meaning and message. Some converts to Christianity were formerly pagan; others were of Jewish heritage. Some early Christian communities were located in Jerusalem; others were located in Asia Minor, Rome, Greece, Syria, Persia, and North Africa. The differences that grew out of varying contexts and locations only intensified and became more pronounced during the patristic-era efforts to formalize Christian doctrine.

It would be an error to think that at one time in Christian history, all Christians agreed about all aspects of their faith and worship. This distinction may prove helpful if it is taken to mean that there is and always has been diversity within the Christian faith, but misleading if it is taken to mean that divisions are so stark that no common beliefs exist. Perhaps the best way to understand this diversity is to consider some of the differences in major Christian communions.

An individual communion has a common set of beliefs, rites (or worship practices), theologies, sacraments, creeds, priesthood or ministerial structures, biblical texts, and more. Often the most important shared belief is an understanding of baptism and the ritual meal of the Eucharist. When churches are in full communion with one another, such as the Evangelical Lutheran Church of America and the Episcopal Church, they not only recognize one another as counterparts of a larger whole (something that might be said of many, if not most, mainline Christian churches) but also have a mutual recognition of baptism and sharing of the Eucharist. When groups do not exist in communion, they see other groups as having significant doctrinal error, faulty or different leadership practices and worship structures, and no binding authority over one another. Many churches recognize some elements of other churches as legitimate while taking issue with other aspects.

Early Christian Diversity

The Jesus movement. The first Christian communities, from roughly 30 to 100 CE, existed without the formal structure of an institutionalized religion. This first community may be properly referred to as the Jesus movement, because initially its members were disciples of Jesus during his lifetime and later were immediate followers of people who had known Jesus in the flesh. Most initial followers of Jesus would have been Palestinian Jews who had listened to Jesus' teachings and whose understanding of their ancestral religion was subsequently transformed. Even among this group, one could find a variety of approaches to Jewish religion and culture. From roughly 175 BCE through the New Testament era, the three major Jewish groups, which the Bible refers to, are the Pharisees (scribes and strict observers of the Law), Sadducees (the priestly class and collaborators with the Roman government), and political revolutionaries, some of whom came to be called "Zealots." Many scholars believe that Pharisaic Judaism produced the majority of early Jewish members of the Jesus movement.

Hellenistic and Roman Christianity. From the second through the early fifth centuries, the Jesus movement advanced in a world mixed with Jewish, pagan, and other influences. The movement changed as it spread beyond its Hebrew heritage into a broader Greco-Roman context. As more and more persons of non-Jewish heritage became followers of the movement, the movement took on a distinctive Hellenistic (Greek) or Roman character. This shift is noticeable in the language that late-first-century Christians began using to describe Jesus, as well as in the nature of the doctrinal debates that flourished in subsequent centuries. A good example is the advance in nonbiblical language to describe the Trinity (e.g., *persona*, *substantia*, and *trinitas*) introduced by Tertullian in the early third century. These nonbiblical terms were heavily relied on in the fourth century to settle questions about the nature of God as three-in-one. Another fine example is Augustine of Hippo in the fourth and fifth century, who imparted Neo-Platonic ideas throughout the corpus of his broadly influential theological writing. Christianity's transition in its first centuries away from its principally Jewish heritage to a movement characterized by a widespread dialogue with Mediterranean culture and philosophy characterized the era of Hellenistic and Roman Christianity.

Diverse attitudes toward women. The Jesus movement was deeply socially transformative. At its inception it appeared to dissolve certain social and class divisions among people, providing new space and status for persons once confined to the margins of religious and social participation. Recorded in the Gospels, Jesus' ministries to the poor, the sick, and the socially "unclean" (prostitutes, tax collectors, menstruant women, and so on) defied conventional boundaries and set the precedent for a more inclusive Christian community. This socially flexible attitude also allowed members of the crafts and merchant classes to take leadership roles that elsewhere would have been reserved for political and financial elites. The early baptismal rule described in Paul's Letter to the Galatians reflects this transformed view of social roles: "For through faith you are all children of God in Christ Jesus. For all of you who were baptized into Christ have clothed yourselves with Christ. There is neither Jew nor Greek, there is neither slave nor free person, there is not male and female; for you are all one in Christ Jesus" (Galatians 3:26–28).

Women, in particular, benefited from the early Jesus movement, because it accommodated and even appears to have advanced the social role of women beyond their normal opportunities in the Greco-Roman world. Although scholars debate the degree to which women assumed leadership at the outset of the Jesus movement, by the end of the first century (evidenced in the later letters of the New Testament such as 1 and 2 Timothy), Christians already were divided about the role women should play.

THE ROLE OF WOMEN: THEN AND NOW

Women represent roughly half of all Christian people, but for most of Christian history, women have not led their church communities as pastors, deacons, priests, elders, bishops, or popes. Historically, and in many church communities even today, women do not vote in church councils, are not educated formally in theology or the study of the Bible, and have had limited opportunity to participate in the official leadership structures of their churches. More far-reaching, the restriction of women's religious participation both reflects and also contributes to biased attitudes toward women in other sociopolitical spheres. In Christian history, much of the restrictions placed on women historically flows from the Bible (and more specifically, from particular ways of reading and interpreting the Bible). As the suffragist Elizabeth Cady Stanton observed in her introduction to *The Woman's Bible* in 1895:

> From the inauguration of the movement for women's emancipation the Bible has been used to hold her in the "divinely ordained sphere," prescribed in the Old and New Testaments.

Continued

Continued

The canon and civil law; church and state; priests and legislators; all political parties and religious denominations have alike taught that woman was made after man, of man, and for man, an inferior being, subject to man. Creeds, codes, Scriptures and statutes, are all based on this idea. The fashions, forms, ceremonies and customs of society, church ordinances and discipline all grow out of this idea. . . .

The Bible teaches that woman brought sin and death into the world, that she precipitated the fall of the race, that she was arraigned before the judgment seat of Heaven, tried, condemned and sentenced. Marriage for her was to be a condition of bondage, maternity a period of suffering and anguish, and in silence and subjection, she was to play the role of a dependent on man's bounty for all her material wants, and for all the information she might desire on vital questions of the hour, she was commanded to ask her husband at home. Here is the Bible position of women briefly summed up.[1]

From the nineteenth century until the present day, Christian theologians have been seeking to understand and improve the role of women in the church. Challenged by ideas such as Stanton's, Christians have explored the range of theological topics, including what Jesus' attitudes were toward women; what the Bible as a whole says about women; how modern people are to interpret derogatory attitudes toward women found in the Bible and elsewhere throughout the theological tradition; what major Christian thinkers of the past said about women; how much authority we should place on past precedent (for example, excluding women from ministry) for today's practice; how we constructively bring women's voices into the theological conversation today; and more.

---

[1] Elizabeth Cady Stanton, *The Woman's Bible: A Classic Feminist Perspective* (Mineola, NY: Dover, 2002), 7.

Continued

The breadth of contemporary scholarship on the role of women in the Christian faith tradition and churches reveals two critical insights about diversity within Christianity: women have played a fascinating and creative (even if little-acknowledged) function in the formation and preservation of Christianity throughout its two-thousand-year history, and Christian men and women in all eras have held an array of ideas about what role women should play. Today the status of women's participation and leadership is one of the more interesting and immediately noticeable aspects of diversity among different Christian worship communions, with some fully embracing women in all ministerial capacities and others retaining restrictions on women.[2]

Gnostic Christianities. Divided attitudes toward women often parallel other aspects and emphases of Christian groups' doctrinal development. For example, among the varieties of early Christian groups (e.g., Marcionists and Valentinians), some believed that Jesus held a special knowledge of the cosmos, to which his followers could gain access. Such groups stressed the spiritual realm over the earthly one. These groups are commonly called Gnostics, deriving their name from the Greek word *gnosis*, meaning "knowledge."

As a result of such emphasis on the spiritual, distinctions in gender, race, and status were even less important to these Christians than to others, and women were often afforded higher status in their circles. Over time, however, both their spiritual doctrines and their admission of women to the highest leadership roles fell into disfavor. During the patristic era, the most prominent Christian leaders ultimately labeled Gnostic opinions heretical and suppressed their beliefs. Because Gnostic writings were preserved mostly in polemical works (in other words, in writings by opponents of Gnosticism), little was known about Gnostic Christianities until a library of Gnostic texts was unearthed in a 1945 excavation in Nag Hammadi, Egypt.

---

[2] For an illuminating history of women in Christianity, consult Rosemary Radford Ruethers's *Women and Redemption: A Theological History* (Minneapolis: Augsburg Fortress, 1998).

AN EARLY CHRISTIAN'S VIEW OF GNOSTICS

Irenaeus, a Christian author of the second century, recounts the beliefs of Gnostic "heretics" in his work *Against Heresies*. The following excerpt from the first chapter of this work details the elaborate levels of divine hierarchy that typified Gnostic systems of belief:

They maintain, then, that in the invisible and ineffable heights above there exists a certain, perfect, pre-existent Aeon, whom they call Proarche, Propator, and Bythus, and describe as being invisible and incomprehensible. Eternal and unbegotten, he remained throughout innumerable cycles of ages in profound serenity and quiescence. There existed along with him Ennoea, whom they also call Charis and Sige. At last this Bythus determined to send forth from himself the beginning of all things, and deposited this production (which he had resolved to bring forth) in his contemporary Sige, even as seed is deposited in the womb. She then, having received this seed, and becoming pregnant, gave birth to Nous, who was both similar and equal to him who had produced him, and was alone capable of comprehending his father's greatness. This Nous they call Monogenes, and Father, and the Beginning of all Things. Along with him was also produced Aletheia; and these four constituted the first and first-begotten Pythagorean Tetrad, which they also denominate the root of all things. For there are first Bythus and Sige, and then Nous and Aletheia. And Monogenes, perceiving for what purpose he had been produced, also himself sent forth Logos and Zoe, after him, and the beginning and fashioning of the entire Pleroma. By the conjunction of Logos and Zoe were brought forth Anthropos and Ecclesia; and thus were formed the first-begotten Ogdoad, the root and substance of all things.[3]

---

[3] Irenaeus, *Against Heresies, in Ante-Nicene Fathers*, ed. Alexander Roberts and James Donaldson (Peabody, MA: Hendrickson, 2004), 1: 316–317.

Early Christian Orthodoxy. Diocletian ruled as emperor of Rome from 284 to 305 CE. For a number of reasons (including the empire's vast size, corruption, and economic concerns), Diocletian decided to split the Roman Empire into eastern and western territories to be ruled by two emperors. One consequence of this political event was the development of two dominant strains of thought throughout the first millennium of Christian history: Eastern and Western. Eastern Christians generally spoke Greek and had theological traditions stemming primarily from the cities of Alexandria and Antioch. The Greek traditions in the fourth century gained influence under Constantine, the first Christian Roman Emperor. Western Christians typically spoke Latin, and their dominant theological centers were located in Rome and Carthage. They retained a sense of primacy over their Eastern counterparts because, they argued, the Bishop of Rome (the pope) was the universal pastor for all the Christian churches by virtue of his historical lineage descending from Jesus' disciple Peter. However, both Eastern and Western Christians considered themselves apostolic, which means they believed their bishops fulfilled an unbroken succession descendant from the first apostles. Eastern and Western Christians participated in doctrinal debates throughout the patristic era, and each considered the other orthodox (conforming to correct, accepted, or traditional doctrine). When conflict arose, the geographic, linguistic, and cultural differences between Eastern and Western Christians often exceeded real doctrinal disagreement.

Branches of Eastern Christianity

The Eastern Christian churches of the patristic era covered a vast range, stretching from Persia and throughout the Mediterranean area, India, and China, geographically outstripping the Western churches. As such, Eastern churches also varied one from another. Some patristic-era churches stood out as unusual in the spectrum of Eastern Christianity; others were doctrinally identical to Western churches but were culturally Eastern, because much of the distinction between Eastern and Western churches could be attributed simply to the political division of the Roman Empire into eastern and western territories.

One prominent early Eastern church was the Church of the East in Sassanid, Persia, which in the early fifth century followed the views of a man named Nestorius. Nestorius held that Jesus' human and divine natures were separate from each other in such a way that there were actually two distinct persons in Jesus. As such, Nestorius argued that Mary could be considered the mother of Jesus but not the mother of God. Nestorius's position, however, was condemned at the Council of Ephesus in 431 and again at Chalcedon in 451, where the majority opinion was that Jesus was one divine person in whom two natures (one human and one divine) coexisted without confusion or change. The anti-Nestorian position became standard in the West. The Eastern Church in Sassanid, however, espoused the views of Nestorius and was hence labeled the Nestorian Church. This church has continued from the fifth century until the present day.

Unlike the Nestorian Church, many Eastern churches developed in doctrinal agreement with the first three ecumenical councils of the patristic era (Council of Nicaea in 325, First Council of Constantinople in 381, and the Council of Ephesus in 431) but rejected the creedal language produced by the councils of the late fifth century and beyond. These churches are known as the Oriental Orthodox churches and have Armenian, Syriac, Coptic, Indian, and Ethiopian varieties. They act in communion with one another and share doctrine but preserve independent leadership structures (and are thus referred to as *autocephalous*, meaning "self-headed"). These churches continue to exist today, maintaining their distinctive ethnic heritages and linguistic cultures.

Still other Eastern churches identify themselves as apostolic and have a history rooted in the earliest Christian period. The first Eastern churches were located in Jerusalem, Antioch, Alexandria, and Constantinople and spread throughout Eastern Europe, Russia, and Greece. Roughly fifteen Eastern Orthodox (or simply Orthodox) churches exist today, each with independent organizational structures and authority, geographical jurisdiction, cultural uniqueness, and ethnic distinctions. The Orthodox churches are equal to one another but honor the church of the Patriarchate of Constantinople as the "first among equals." The Orthodox churches of the present day share a common doctrine rooted in the major ecumenical councils of the patristic era, as well as the belief that they carry the legacy and lineage of the first Christian church established by Jesus.

For the first millennium after Christ, the Orthodox churches remained in communion with the Western churches. However, relations were often tense. Among the contentious issues were the role and authority of the Roman pope over the Eastern churches, determination of whether territories were properly to be called Western or Eastern, disputes over the language of the Nicene Creed pertaining to the nature of the Trinity, the proper manner of worship in church liturgy, whether priests could marry, and whether churches could have icons for the faithful to venerate. Long-mounting tensions over these issues came to a head in 1054 when the Eastern Patriarch Michael Cerularius and the Roman Pope Leo IX feuded over church practices. The feud escalated, with the heads of both churches mutually excommunicating each other. This event is known as the Eastern Schism (also called the East–West Schism and the Great Schism). Divisions between Eastern and Western Christians worsened during the Crusades of the eleventh through the thirteenth centuries. Since the mid-twentieth century, however, an ongoing dialogue between the Eastern Orthodox and Roman Catholic churches has striven toward restoration of full communion between the two.

Despite the schism, more than twenty Eastern churches remain nonschismatic (or in full communion) with the Western churches and recognize the primacy of the Bishop of Rome. These churches, referred to as the Eastern Catholic Churches, variously have always remained in communion with Rome or have returned to communion from a prior schism.

The Christians of Saint Thomas comprise yet another Eastern church. Originally situated off the Malabar Coast of India, this group claims to have been founded by the Apostle Thomas in the mid-first century. Geographically insulated for centuries, these believers are one of the oldest Eastern Christian varieties.

As a group, Eastern churches encompass a range of worship models or liturgical rites. Some common aspects of Eastern Christianity include observing seven sacraments, allowing men to marry before becoming priests, practicing chrismation (or anointing with sacred oil) immediately after baptism, and emphasizing salvation as divinization of the human.

Roman Catholic Christianity

Roman Catholic Christianity (often simply called Roman Catholicism), like Eastern Orthodox Christianity, believes itself to be the
ongoing presence of the original church established by Jesus and
his apostles. Catholics believe that the historical connection of the
modern church to the original church is guaranteed by the apostolic
succession of bishops, who fulfill an unbroken lineage to the first
disciples. The Roman Catholic Church further argues for a continuity
of Catholic doctrine from the time of Jesus to the present. This legacy
is believed to be guaranteed and carried on by the church leaders
through their special teaching authority, called the magisterium.

Just as the Eastern traditions reflect the cultural influences of
the Eastern Roman Empire, so Roman Catholicism reflects the
cultural heritage and history of the Western Roman Empire. Catholic worship had been conducted in Latin throughout the world for
centuries, a carryover from the Catholic Church's ties to Rome. Even
today, Latin is used for many important Roman Catholic documents.
The Vatican, housing the pope's residence and the administrative
center of the Roman Catholic Church, is located in Vatican City, an
independent territory within the city of Rome.

Rome is vital in Roman Catholicism because Catholics believe
that the church in Rome was established by Jesus' disciple Peter.
Catholic teaching traces to Matthew 16:18–19 the belief that Peter's
church in particular has central significance for Christians. In the
passage, Jesus says to Peter:

> And so I say to you, you are Peter, and upon this rock I will
> build my church, and the gates of the netherworld shall not
> prevail against it. I will give you the keys to the kingdom
> of heaven. Whatever you bind on earth shall be bound in
> heaven; and whatever you loose on earth shall be loosed
> in heaven.

Based on these verses (which are interpreted differently by other
Christian churches), the argument proceeds that Peter and his
apostolic successors have unique authority and responsibility in
the Catholic Church. As Bishop of Rome, the pope is heir to this
legacy. Although all bishops of the Roman Catholic Church have a

VATICAN COUNCIL II

In 1959 Pope John XXIII announced that he was convening an international ecumenical council of bishops. He hoped among other things to deepen the spiritual life of the church, address conditions of the modern world, update the code of canon law, invite separated Christians to renewed unity with the Catholic Church, and further enlighten all Christians. The spirit of the council was characterized by the Italian word *aggiornamento*, meaning "bringing up to date." Many of the pope's closest advisers were concerned about the effect such an updating would have on the church. Indeed, the council proved to be the most profound renewal of the church in four centuries.

The council was difficult to initiate, organize, and manage due to the logistical challenges of working with thousands of bishops, their aides, and staff all at once. In addition, Pope John XXIII died and was succeeded by Paul VI in 1963, right in the middle of the council. Despite such challenges, the council successfully convened in four sessions from 1962 to 1965, producing a number of major and authoritative documents that reflected and helped bring a renewed sense of the Roman Catholic Church's vigor, vibrancy, engagement, openness, and service in the modern world.

collegial (or equal and mutual) relationship to one another in Roman Catholicism, they nevertheless stand under the ultimate authority of the pope, who is considered the universal pastor of the Catholic Church. The pope is afforded unique doctrinal authority in the Catholic Church in its teaching on infallibility, proclaimed by the First Vatican Council in 1870, which argues that the pope speaks without error (infallibly) when he does so on behalf of the church in matters of faith and morals.

Structurally, Catholic churches are led by local priests, and sometimes lay (or nonordained) administrators, who often are accompanied by a staff of lay ministers and sometimes deacons (ordained men who may be married). Churches are organized in regional clusters called dioceses. Bishops lead dioceses and participate in dialogue with one another at the regional and national levels. For example, the U.S. Conference of Catholic Bishops (USCCB) produces materials and instructions (sometimes based on Vatican direction) for American Catholics. Occasionally, bishops convene an international ecumenical council, as with the 1962–1965 Second Vatican Council. Through the collegial dialogue of bishops, councils provide guidance to the pope on the direction of the Roman Catholic Church. Most often, however, the pope is counseled by his College of Cardinals, bishops appointed by a pope to a lifetime of special service and advisement. When a pope dies, the College of Cardinals convenes in a conclave to elect a new Bishop of Rome. The overall church leadership structure is referred to as the hierarchy.

The hierarchy is one defining feature of the Roman Catholic Church with respect to other Christian communions. Other characteristics include the observance of seven sacraments, the celibacy of the priesthood, ordained religious orders of men, lay religious orders of men and women, infant baptism, and confirmation during adolescence (the latter two features, regarding baptism and confirmation, are not the exclusive practice but the norm).

Protestant Groups of the Reformation and Beyond

The Protestant Reformation was a reform movement in Western Europe wherein key theologians and heads of state rejected key teachings and practices, as well as the governing authority, of the Roman Catholic Church and established independent national churches. At the outset, the Reformation was not a single, consolidated movement with a charter and a theological agenda. Rather, it began as an organic movement that snowballed due to varying political situations, geographic locations, charismatic leaders, and other changes that came as reform movements gained histories of their own. The theological disputes among Protestant groups were often as significant as those between Protestants and Catholics.

Principal groupings of Reformation Protestant churches or movements included the following:

REFORMATION CHURCH	KEY FIGURES	START DATE	LOCATION	OFFSHOOTS
Lutheran	Martin Luther	1517	Germany	Pietism movement
Church of England/ Anglican	Henry VIII	1534	England	Society of Friends (Quakers) Episcopalian Baptist Methodist
Anabaptist	Thomas Munzer Nicholas Storch Conrad Grebel Felix Manz George Blaurock	1525	Germany The Netherlands Switzerland England	Mennonite Amish
Calvinist/ Reformed	John Calvin	1536	Switzerland	Church of Scotland Presbyterian

Christian denominations resulting from the Reformation have continued to multiply in the past four centuries and today enjoy staggering numbers. The *Dictionary of Christianity in America* recognizes more than 20,000 different Christian churches in America today. This number is so large, in part, because of a freedom from organizational structure and the impulse to reform, both of which have characterized Protestant churches since the sixteenth century. Unattached to the formal structures and long histories of the Roman Catholic or Eastern Orthodox churches, Protestant churches never developed the same leadership controls characteristic of the older orders. Moreover, the older orders acted, to varying degrees, in accord with the ancient monarchies of Europe. As monarchies were replaced by democratic governments, an unprecedented religious freedom followed. The democratic impulse in political governance was mirrored by a diversity of new religious communities.

Many Protestant churches today have their denominational roots in the Reformation, but many others are more recent expressions resulting either from further church schisms or simply from newfound inspirations or movements. The following list of Protestant Christian sects that have emerged since the sixteenth-century Papal Schism is by no means exhaustive:

Adventist Christians	Evangelical Lutheran Church
Amish	in America
Anabaptists	Fundamentalist Christians
Anglican Christians	Holiness Churches
Apostolic Christians	Independent or nondenomina-
Assemblies of God	tional Christian churches
Baptist Christians	Jehovah's Witness
Brethren	Lutheran Church–Missouri
Charismatic Christians	Synod
Christian and Missionary	Mennonites
Alliance	Methodist Christians
Christian Science	Pentecostal Christians
Church of Christ	Pietist Christians
Church of God	Plymouth Brethren
Church of Jesus Christ	Presbyterians
of Latter Day Saints	Quakers
Church of the Nazarene	Reformed
Congregationalist	Shakers
Christians	Unitarian Christians
Disciples of Christ	United Church of Christ
Evangelical Christians	United Methodist

Each group has its own structure, statement of faith, practice for ordaining or recognizing leadership, worship models, understandings of Scripture, and more. Were one to study any group or denomination on this list, it would quickly become clear that some hold widely shared doctrines, while others are so idiosyncratic that the majority of the other groups would not consider them truly "Christian." Christian communions debate whether some of these are "churches" or "cults." Such debates reflect the ongoing tension within Christian churches over right doctrine, leadership, spirituality, organization, and practice.

THE PENTECOSTAL AND CHARISMATIC MOVEMENTS TODAY

In the late nineteenth century, the United States witnessed fervent religious revivals among poor and working-class people, who felt dissatisfied with the lack of apparent godliness in the mainline churches. This "holiness Christian" movement, motivated by the writings of John Wesley (1703–1791), emerged as a response to this perceived deficit in the mainline churches. This movement aimed at intensifying Christian godliness and derived its inspiration from the New Testament community as described in the book of Acts and Paul's letters in the Bible. Holiness Christians asserted that the New Testament church prominently featured the Holy Spirit as energizing, inspiring, and guiding Christian worship and practice. Based on this New Testament model, Holiness Christians began seeking greater personal inspiration, fueled by the "baptism by the Holy Spirit." They believed proof of such baptism was found in the manifestation of spiritual gifts (such as those described in 1 Corinthians chapters 12–14) in their lives.

At the beginning of the twentieth century, key Holiness preachers such as Charles Parham (1901) and William Seymour (1906) popularized the notion that baptism by the Holy Spirit was demonstrated through the gift of glossolalia, or speaking in tongues. They derived this concept from Acts 2:1–4, which describes the birth of the Christian church. The context for this passage is that the eleven apostles of Jesus have witnessed Jesus' ascension into heaven and have reconvened in Jerusalem to select a member to replace

Continued

Continued

Judas (who betrayed Jesus). They select Matthias and wait fifty days (the fiftieth day being the "Pentecost," a word that comes from a Greek term meaning "fiftieth day").

> When the time for Pentecost was fulfilled, they were all in one place together. And suddenly there came from the sky a noise like a strong driving wind, and it filled the entire house in which they were. Then there appeared to them tongues as of fire, which parted and came to rest on each one of them. And they were all filled with the holy Spirit and began to speak in different tongues, as the Spirit enabled them to proclaim.

Parham and Seymour quickly spread the message of baptism by the Holy Spirit and speaking in tongues in their new Pentecostal movement through the establishment of missions, churches, and camp meetings. Their preaching and message had wide appeal and grew rapidly and exponentially throughout the United States and the world at large during the twentieth century. As of today, there are nearly six hundred million Pentecostal Christians, composing one of the largest denominations worldwide.

From the middle of the twentieth century until today, the success of the Pentecostal churches has been an inspiration to nearly every mainline Christian denomination. Though they do not all seek the gift of glossolalia, churches globally are adopting and preaching a more vital sense of the presence and role of the Holy Spirit in the life of their communities. The term *charismatic* (derived from the Greek *charisma*, meaning "gift") describes this modern movement.

Charismatic Christians may belong to any denomination or they may be independent, nondenominational Christians. They share a common sense that the Holy Spirit is active, present, and propelling Christians into more energetic and vigorous applications of their faith in the world. Together, the Charismatic and Pentecostal movements are arguably the most transformative development in Christianity in the past one hundred years.

Ecumenical Movement

Given the many, diverse Orthodox, Catholic, and Protestant Christian churches today with often strongly divergent belief systems, one might ask how such groups understand one another and why they do not just join together as one Christian church. These questions take on a sense of urgency in light of the impulse for unity among Christians expressed in the New Testament. The earliest Christian communities highly valued unity in theory, even if they were not able to achieve it in practice. Two thousand years later, doctrinal differences, cultural flavors, linguistic factors, and geographic boundaries have produced an astounding number of Christianities, professing related but diverse beliefs.

One recent approach to addressing this diversity is the ecumenical movement. Ecumenism is the effort by Christians to reunify. Churches participating in ecumenism are driven by a sense that human beings often err, especially at the institutional level. Among the greatest of errors is the historical separation of Christians from one another, a separation that too often has been accompanied by violence or war. Ecumenically minded Christians believe that the Universal Church is always in need of renewal and is always led by the Holy Spirit. As such, they argue that gifts of the Spirit given to one community may be absent from another. Thus the full potential of the Christian people, united as church, can be realized only as a whole.

Although many Christian churches aspire to ecumenism, theological divisions are not easily overcome simply because a spirit of mutuality among groups has emerged. Furthermore, some church groups have no desire to participate in the ecumenical movement.

The ecumenical movement takes different forms. Sometimes churches undertake numerous dialogues with several other denominations simultaneously. Churches may also enter into bilateral dialogues, in which leaders of two separate church communions convene to discuss issues and address historical grievances. Bilateral dialogues, for example, could take place between Catholics and Orthodox, or between Baptists and Lutherans. Multilateral dialogue opportunities can also occur in wider forums, such as the World Council of Churches (WCC), a fellowship of more than three hundred churches. In the WCC, church leaders and theologians convene yearly to discuss specific aspects of faith, worship, and Christian life. Often Christians join together through social justice and service acts. Though some in the ecumenical movement strive for full unification, others prefer half steps and modest goals for advancing ecumenical relations. Examples of such ecumenical activities include common prayer in nonsacramental worship, concelebration of weddings, and service programs.

Conclusion

Christian variety is as old as Christianity itself. Within a single church, one will find differences of opinion. Among different church families, there are often prominent differences with deep historical roots. Major differences may be grasped first by asking whether a specific group is Eastern, Orthodox, Catholic, or Protestant. Second, by asking questions about the group's location, heritage, history, and connections to other Christian churches, one may gain insight into the nature of the belief and worship structures of the church. Third, one should study the statements of faith, leadership structures, and worship practices of the church to understand how it lives out its identity as a Christian church.

Ultimately how does one determine the boundaries for acceptable Christian community? Is belief in Jesus as God and savior according to the Bible sufficient, as it is for membership in the WCC? Must one have certain worship practices, such as the observance of a specific number of sacraments? Must one have certain interpretations of Scripture, such as the literal approach to the Bible taken by Holiness churches of Appalachia, who demonstrate their faith by handling serpents, as is mentioned in Scripture (see Mark 16:18)? Must one recognize the supreme leadership of the pope, or, conversely, reject that leadership?

Such questions are in fact the reason for much of the historical diversity within Christianity. In the past, different answers sometimes led to dire conflicts between groups. Today the ecumenical movement gives reason to hope that a sense of charity and unity will prevail over historical differences. Despite diversity in doctrine, leadership, or readings of the Bible, Christians strive to find mutual ways to live their common values of service and justice.

Questions for Discussion and Review

1. Describe differences among the first Christian communities. What were some contributing factors to these differences?

2. On what grounds do you think early Christian theologians justified naming some beliefs "orthodox" and others "heretical"? What might Christianity look like today if these judgments were reversed?

3. Name the various branches of Eastern Christianity. What is the relationship of each to the Roman Catholic Church?

4. What are the two major schisms in the history of the Roman Catholic Church?

5. Describe distinctive elements of the Roman Catholic Church hierarchy. Is the passage in the Gospel of Matthew quoted in this chapter persuasive regarding the primacy of the pope over all of Christendom? Explain.

6. Many Protestant groups are identified in this chapter. Why are there so many different groups?

7. What experience, if any, have you had of diverse Christian groups? What do you think were or are major points of contrast in belief or practice in those groups?

8. Describe the ecumenical movement. What is your opinion on the value of Christian reunification? What might be some effective strategies for advancing unity? What are some of the obstacles?

9. Briefly research two or more Christian groups cited in this chapter. Chart their origins, major points of contrast, and commonalities. Then consider what steps the groups might take to overcome their differences.

Key Terms

apostolic

autocephalous

cardinal

Charismatic

chrismation

collegial

communion

conclave

deacon

diocese

Eastern Catholic

Eastern Orthodox

ecumenical

excommunicate

"first among equals"

Gnostic

Hellenistic

infallibility

Jesus movement

lay

magisterium

Nag Hammadi

Nestorian

polemical

pope

Reformed

rite

Sassanid Church
of Persia

universal pastor

Resources

Angold, Michael, ed. *History of Christianity*. Vol. 5, *Eastern Christianity*. Cambridge, MA: Cambridge University Press, 2006.

Kelly, Joseph F. *The Ecumenical Councils of the Catholic Church: A History*. Collegeville, MN: Liturgical Press, 2009.

McGrath, Alister. *Christianity's Dangerous Idea: The Protestant Revolution: A History from the Sixteenth Century to the Twenty-First*. New York: HarperCollins, 2007.

Murphy, Francesca Aran, and Christopher Asprey, eds. *Ecumenism Today*. Hampshire, UK, and Burlington, VT: Ashgate, 2008.

Parry, Ken, ed. *The Blackwell Companion to Eastern Christianity*. Oxford, UK: Blackwell, 2010.

Vidmar, John. *The Catholic Church through the Ages: A History*. Mahwah, NJ: Paulist Press, 2005.

6 Christian Worship and Practice

CHAPTER

WHAT TO EXPECT

This chapter introduces major aspects of Christian worship and spiritual practice. The following categories are discussed:

- worship in prayer
- worship in liturgy
- liturgical year and Christian holidays
- the Virgin Mary, saints, and martyrs
- social service and outreach
- religious orders

What Is Christian Spirituality?

Today one commonly hears the phrase, "I'm spiritual but not religious." This statement suggests a distinction between organized approaches to religion and a more innate or personal, even if less defined, awareness of God or the divine. Indeed, religious experience can be highly unstructured and individualized. At the same time, however, spirituality may fruitfully be structured and channeled within a religion and its theological system of belief. In this sense, spirituality may refer broadly to the global and encompassing way that people feel, experience, and live out their religious faith.

Religious spirituality is lived formally and informally, communally and individually, boldly and subtly throughout all aspects of life. Participating in ritual services on special days, reciting statements of belief, praying: these are just a sampling of ways people may participate in religion. People may also structure their life and work, such as their approach to marriage or career or volunteer work, according to the tenets of their religion. People may journey to places their religion holds significant or sacred. All ways that people live their religious beliefs may be examples of spirituality.

Christian spirituality refers to the breadth and depth of how faith is lived and experienced by Christian believers, in both historical and contemporary contexts, by individuals and within larger church communities. The range of Christian spiritual practices, as with all aspects of Christianity, is wide and varied. Although Christianity has as many approaches to spirituality as it does churches and people, all genuinely Christian spirituality will be rooted in the person of Jesus. This means first and foremost attending to the story and example of Jesus' life as recorded in the Bible. Second, it means being inspired by the Holy Spirit to live a life of service to others in imitation of Christ. Third, it means living in community with others so as to join one's individual life with one's own church community (and more broadly, with all Christians as one Body of Christ). Though Christian spirituality takes many forms, it always shares the Christocentric (or Christ-centered) elements of charity, gifts, and community.

Charity

The most important commonality in Christian spirituality is Christian charity, or in Latin, *caritas*. This charity refers to the self-giving love Jesus shows in the New Testament. Because Christians hold Jesus as the model for how all human beings should live, they attempt to model their spiritual practice on Jesus' self-sacrificing service to others. The moral instruction of the New Testament encourages Christians to follow Christ's example of offering service and gift without expectation of reward or compensation. The book of Acts (see 2:44–45), for example, describes Christians as living communally so they may collectively help to meet each other's basic material needs. In the First Letter of John (see 3:16–18), Christians are instructed to meet one another's material needs as a sign of their love of God.

Early Christians believed it impossible to love the unseen God without loving the people who were right before their eyes. Moreover, they believed that loving people means more than having kind

CHRISTIAN CHARITY

Christian charity entails concrete acts of service and gift. For example, consider the use of material wealth in the following two biblical examples.

1 John 3:16–18

The way we came to know love was that he laid down his life for us; so we ought to lay down our lives for our brothers. If someone who has worldly means sees a brother in need and refuses him compassion, how can the love of God remain in him? Children, let us not love in word or speech but in deed and truth.

Acts 2:44–47

All who believed were together and had all things in common; they would sell their property and possessions and divide them among all according to each one's need. Every day they devoted to meeting together in the temple area and to breaking bread in their homes. They ate their meals with exultation and sincerity of heart, praising God and enjoying favor with all the people. And every day the Lord added to their number those who were being saved.

feelings toward one another; it means serving one another for the flourishing of the whole human family. At base, Christian charity requires Christians to meet one another's needs for food, clothing, shelter, and so on. This charity differs from romantic love or the love among family members and friends; it is the fundamental compassion for and active service to all human beings that is required of Christians. This concept of charity serves as the foundation for Christian ethics and social justice. Thus Christian faith emphasizes loving everyone, even one's enemy, through actions that promote the other's welfare.

Gifts

Another key aspect of Christian spirituality is the notion of spiritual gifts, or charisms. Early Christians recognized that people are graced with different abilities and ways of serving one another, and thereby serving God. Christianity holds, in its doctrine of creation, that all people are created with an inherent purpose and dignity. The skills unique to each person, therefore, are blessings to be returned in service to others. One person might have a gift for science, another for singing, a third for teaching, and so on. Each gift is an expression of a person's God-given uniqueness, and all gifts may be applied in service.

Christian spirituality recognizes the diversity of human gifts and sees in every gift the potential for charitable service to God

UNITY IN DIVERSITY

In Paul's First Letter to the Corinthians, the author speaks of the diversity of spiritual gifts even as he emphasizes the unity of community that all such gifts serve.

1 Corinthians 12:4–11

There are different kinds of spiritual gifts but the same Spirit; there are different kinds of service but the same Lord; there are different workings but the same God who produces all of them in everyone. To each individual the manifestation of the Spirit is given for some benefit. To one is given through the Spirit the expression of wisdom; to another the expression of knowledge according to the same Spirit; to another faith by the same Spirit; to another gifts of healing by the one Spirit; to another mighty deeds; to another prophecy; to another discernment of spirits; to another varieties of tongues; to another interpretation of tongues. But one and the same Spirit produces all of these, distributing them individually to each person as he wishes.

and neighbor. All gifts, whether individual or shared, must be used according to the guiding principles of faith, hope, and love, which are considered the three theological virtues. When separated from these virtues, gifts may become distorted and lose value. When guided by these virtues, however, all gifts find expression in service to the human family.

Community

A third common element of Christian spirituality is the principle of community. From the beginning of the Christian era, adherents saw themselves as having a corporate existence. They called themselves collectively the Body of Christ and the People of God, and individually brothers and sisters. They recognized that through their baptism, they had joined a family of believers, sometimes called a messianic family.

CHRISTIANS AS ONE BODY

In several places in the New Testament, the authors use the metaphor of the body to describe what the Christian community is like. Just as body parts act together to form a whole, so Christians work together to form a church community. In 1 Corinthians (12:12—13:13), Paul notes that all body parts are needed for the good of the whole. The foot should not be displeased because it is not the eye or the ear. In the same way, he suggests, people should not be jealous or alienated from one another on account of station, talent, or gifts. This metaphor of the body is repeated in the Letter to the Ephesians (5:22–33), in which the author states that Christ is to the church as the head is to its body, and a man is to his wife as the head is to its body.

Both scriptural uses of the metaphor of the body invite the reader to think about the integrative nature of community, of God and the church, and of spouses. However, both also suggest

Continued

Continued

hierarchy in the Body of Christ. In 1 Corinthians, people are dif-
ferentiated on account of their spiritual gifts; some therefore naturally have a higher station than others. In Ephesians, men have a
higher station than women, which is underlined by the comparison
of the male to Christ and the female to the church. The integrative
and holistic implications of the body metaphor may seem to be
compromised by the hierarchical arrangement of persons based
on talent or gender that it implies. Still, both passages soften such
implications by suggesting that love is the guiding principle in
applying spiritual gifts and in mutual service between spouses.

The metaphor of the body was vital, symbolizing the idea that
diverse persons, like different parts of the body, work together to
form a whole. Early Christians placed the value of being a part of
the family of believers even before their biological families. The
family of believers was open to all people, regardless of race, class,
or gender. Moreover, it offered hope that through the life of Jesus,
all people would one day unite and heal the rifts and conflicts that
divided them.

The community is clearly an important element in Christian
spirituality. Though Christians act as individuals in their lives and
work, they also commonly see their work as an aspect of their service to the community as a whole. Especially within the church,
Christians work together to maximize their gifts and efforts on
behalf of others.

Worship in Prayer

Christian communities call their devotional acts and observances
worship. *Worship* as a noun usually refers to communal acts of
devotion, such as a church service or holiday observance. As a verb,
worship typically means to honor or revere, as a divine being or
supernatural power. *Worship* may also refer to what one does when
praising God through any variety of more secular activities, as in, "I

worship God through my work as a pediatrician." Two of the most important expressions of worship are prayer and liturgy.

Prayer derives from the Latin root *precari*, meaning "to beg or beseech." The Hebrew Old Testament and the Christian New Testament both mention prayer frequently. The Bible often refers to people praying publicly and also includes many prayers. Indeed, the biblical book of Psalms is an ancient prayer book. In the New Testament, Christian prayer is modeled on Jesus' many acts of prayer; his best-known prayer is the Lord's Prayer, recorded in the Gospel of Matthew (see 6:9–13) and the Gospel of Luke (see 11:2–4). In the slightly longer Matthew version, Jesus also teaches that people should not make a grand show of devotions and good deeds, because their public performance then becomes its own reward. Rather, he instructs people to pray and do good quietly so that any rewards will be in heaven, not on earth. Following this instruction, Jesus says in Matthew 6:9–13:

> "This is how you are to pray:
>> Our Father in heaven,
>>> hallowed be your name,
>>> your kingdom come,
>>> your will be done, on earth as in heaven.
>> Give us today our daily bread;
>> and forgive us our debts,
>>> as we forgive our debtors;
>> and do not subject us to the final test,
>>> but deliver us from the evil one."

The Lord's Prayer is a good starting place to consider the nature of Christian prayer. The term *prayer* suggests supplication or entreaty before God, and Christians use many forms of prayer in worship. One can pray as a manner of praising God ("hallowed be your name"), as in the Lord's Prayer. One can also pray as a manner of petitioning God to intercede on behalf of human affairs ("Give us this day our daily bread"). Prayer may also be offered to thank God for blessings or express contrition for wrongs. The different intentions behind specific types of prayer inform when and how prayers are offered.

PSALMS: POETRY AND PRAYER

The Psalms is a biblical book of poetry. Scholars believe the biblical Israelites used these psalms as sung prayers in worship. Predominant themes in Psalms include praise of Yahweh (God), lamentation, and priestly prayer. The twenty-third psalm, below, attributed to King David, is among the most celebrated because of its comforting words and bucolic or rustic imagery reflecting the pastoral life of the ancient Israelites.

> The Lord is my shepherd;
>> there is nothing I lack.
>
> In green pastures you let me graze;
>> to safe waters you lead me;
>> you restore my strength.
>
> You guide me along the right path
>> for the sake of your name.
>
> Even when I walk through a dark valley,
>> I fear no harm for you are at my side;
>> your rod and staff give me courage.
>
> You set a table before me
>> as my enemies watch;
>
> You anoint my head with oil;
>> my cup overflows.
>
> Only goodness and love will pursue me
>> all the days of my life;
>
> I will dwell in the house of the Lord
>> for years to come.

Prayer may be individual or communal. Individual prayer is private and may be formal or informal in nature. Examples of individual prayer that is informal would be a student praying before an exam or a job applicant praying on the eve of an interview. An example of a formal individual prayer would be a person praying the Lord's Prayer during an evening meditation. Communal prayer is public, shared by two or more, and it too may be formal or informal. An example of a communal, informal prayer would be a family saying grace before eating. An example of a communal, formal prayer would be the prayers of a church community during Sunday worship.

Christians also pray in many ways. Sometimes prayer is spoken out loud or even sung, while other times it is wordless and experienced as a silent meditation or visualization. Prayer may involve an icon (or religious image) upon which a person meditates or to which a person expresses special devotion. Sometimes prayer has content, using words, images, or passages from the Bible as the subject matter. Other times prayer is without content, as the one praying attempts to empty his or her mind in order merely to be in the presence of God. Some prayer, following in the tradition of Christian mysticism, attempts to elevate the one praying to union with God.

CHRISTIAN MYSTICISM

Prayerful contemplation of the divine is part of the mystical tradition within Christian spirituality. *Mystical* refers to nonconceptual ways of preparing the prayerful person for experiencing the divine. Put another way, the mystical tradition strives to bring the Christian into union with God or into the presence of God, even while it recognizes that God exceeds the human's ability to know or perceive or understand. A wealth of literature exists by Christian mystics describing the processes of prayer and meditation whereby one can know God in this most intimate, even if inexpressible, way. Notable examples of Christian mystics include Francis of Assisi (1182–1226), Catherine of Sienna (1347–1380), Teresa of Ávila (1515–1582), John of the Cross (1542–1591), Thérèse of Lisieux (1873–1897), and Thomas Merton (1915–1968). Following is a passage from a work called *The Mystical Theology*,

Continued

Continued

by the fifth- or sixth-century writer known as Pseudo-Dionysius.[1] It captures the essence of the Christian effort to put into words that which is unfathomable:

> Again, as we climb higher we say this. It is not soul or mind, nor does it possess imagination, conviction, speech, or understanding. Nor is it speech per se, understanding per se. It cannot be spoken of and it cannot be grasped by understanding. It is not number or order, greatness or smallness, equality or inequality, similarity or dissimilarity. It is not immovable, moving, or at rest. It has no power, it is not power, nor is it light. It does not live nor is it life. It is not a substance, nor is it eternity or time. It cannot be grasped by the understanding since it is neither knowledge nor truth. It is not kingship. It is not wisdom. It is neither one nor oneness, divinity nor goodness. Nor is it a spirit, in the sense in which we understand that term. It is not sonship or fatherhood and it is nothing known to us or to any other being. It falls neither within the predicate of nonbeing nor of being. Existing beings do not know it as it actually is and it does not know them as they are. There is no speaking of it, nor name nor knowledge of it. Darkness and light, error and truth—it is none of these. It is beyond assertion and denial. We make assertions and denials of what is next to it, but never of it, for it is beyond every assertion, being the perfect and unique cause of all things, and by virtue of its preeminently simple and absolute nature, free of every limitation, beyond every limitation, it is also beyond denial.

In all these ways, Christians attempt to place themselves in proper relationship to God through praise, lament, petition, contemplation, adoration, and thanksgiving. Christians use prayer as a way

---

[1] *Pseudo-Dionysius: The Complete Works* (New York and Mahwah, NJ: Paulist Press, 1987), 141.

to receive the Holy Spirit and also to entreat God to be more fully present in their lives. Whether offered individually or communally, prayer is a regular and important part of any Christian spirituality.

Worship in Liturgy

One of the most important venues for Christian prayer is the formal worship setting, called liturgy. Liturgies, also called services, are public acts of worship enacted by Christian church communities. Liturgies take place in the churches or sacred spaces where Christian communities meet. The following overview of the components of liturgical worship lends insight into its nature:

Rites. Ritualized and structured actions, usually accompanied by prescribed words, that the church community takes and recites for specific reasons at specific times of the year.

Repetition. Rites are typically orderly and follow prescribed behaviors that are always repeated in the same order as the ritual is performed. Many rites are practiced regularly throughout the year. Others are practiced only on special holy days. Still others are reserved for special events in the life cycle, such as marriage, baptism, or death.

Clergy. Many Christian communities have ordained priests, deacons, presbyters, or ministers who lead worship. These individuals are distinguished from the rest of the congregation, sometimes called the laity, by virtue of their ordination. Ordination is the process by which one becomes an official minister in the church. It usually follows some scholarly and ministerial education and preparation and also typically involves the laying on of hands of other church leaders as a sign of blessing and God's calling the newly ordained to service. Different church communions vary as to whether they ordain both women and men as clergy.

Vestments. Persons conducting or celebrating liturgies often wear ceremonial clothing, whose colors, shapes, and patterns signify and communicate spiritual messages. For example, the alb (a full-length white robe signifying the purity of baptism) is often worn by

Christian ministers and priests leading worship services. Christian ministers will also often wear a stole, which is a long strip of cloth several inches wide that drapes across the celebrant's shoulders and hangs down the front of the alb. The colors, embroidery, and design of the stole signify different festivals, celebrations, or holidays.

Sacraments. These are the highest moments of Christian worship (see chapter 4), with the single most important among them being the celebration of the Eucharist.

Sacramentals. Objects (e.g. candles, incense burners) or actions (e.g. praying, blessing) that serve to enhance the sacred quality of a formal ritual.

Liturgical year. Christian rituals follow a yearly calendar, organized around holy days (holidays), that guides what rituals are performed. A variety of different vestments, colors, readings, and practices are used throughout the liturgical year.

Lectionary. A book of readings that follows the liturgical year. Readings or lections from the Bible often play an important role in Christian rituals.

Music. Christian rituals are frequently accompanied by music, such as the singing of psalms, hymns, and prayer. Hymnals are books of music, which are commonly made available to the congregation so everyone can join in the music of the worship service.

Altar. Many Christian churches have a large table, or altar, which serves as the central place for the celebration of the Eucharist.

Host and chalice. Bread and wine (sometimes grape juice), or the foods used during the Eucharistic liturgy (celebration of the Lord's Supper), are believed to communicate the body and blood of Christ to those who receive the sacrament. The bread, called the host, is typically a round, unleavened wafer made of wheat flour. The wine is frequently presented in a goblet, called a chalice.

Christian liturgies differ from church to church. Many will include all of these elements in their official worship services; others incorporate only some of them.

Liturgical Year and Holidays

Throughout the liturgical year, Christians pay special attention both to the seasons and to holidays or feast days. In both the Eastern and Western traditions, the dates of some major seasons of the liturgical calendar are moveable, which means they vary from year to year. This is the case, for example, with Lent and Easter. On the civil calendar, the dates of these holidays are determined by the lunisolar calendar (based on the position of the moon relative to the sun from month to month). Various church communions may celebrate major Christian holidays on different days, depending on which calendar system is used to determine the dates of major holidays. There is general agreement, however, on the order and basic time of year in which the celebration of key events and liturgical seasons in the Christian system should occur. These include Advent, Christmas, Ordinary Time (following Epiphany), Lent, Triduum, Easter, and Ordinary Time (after Pentecost).

Advent ➡ Christmas ➡ Ordinary Time ➡ Lent ➡ Triduum ➡ Easter ➡ Ordinary Time

Advent. The first season of the liturgical year, Advent begins four Sundays before Christmas. This is a period of waiting, as it demarcates the weeks leading up to the birth of Christ. It is often symbolized by somber colors, such as purple, as the Christian community anticipates the coming of its Savior.

Christmas. This season celebrates the birth of Jesus. It begins on the evening of December 24 and lasts variously through Epiphany on January 6 (celebrating the visit of the Magi to see the infant Jesus) or through the Sunday after Epiphany (celebrating Jesus' baptism). White vestments are commonly worn during Christmas. Christmas Day is December 25.

Ordinary Time. The first period of Ordinary Time in the liturgical year follows Epiphany. *Ordinary* derives from the Latin word *ordo*, which simply refers to "a series or a line." *Ordinary* here, as in ordinal, means the counting of the weeks until Lent begins. The colors green and gold are frequently used in ordinary time.

Lent. This is the season of fasting (a restricted diet, with abstinence from certain foods), almsgiving (giving money, goods, time, and services to those in need), and penance (acts of contrition). Lent stretches from Ash Wednesday to the Triduum (to be discussed next). The season of Lent lasts roughly forty days (not including Sundays) before Easter. On Ash Wednesday, which follows the often exuberant Mardi Gras festivities of the Tuesday before, many persons have their foreheads marked with ash to symbolize human mortality and the need for repentance. Lent concludes on the Thursday evening before Easter, which starts the Triduum. Though the season of Lent is penitential, Sundays are still considered days of celebration. This is especially true for Palm Sunday (the Sunday before Easter), which celebrates Jesus' triumphal arrival in Jerusalem and also anticipates his ultimate Crucifixion a mere week later. Purple is associated with Lent, while red is often used in Palm Sunday worship.

Triduum. This refers to the three-day period (*tri* means "three" and *dies* means "day") before Easter Sunday. The Thursday, called Maundy Thursday (derived from the Latin word *mandatum*, meaning "command"), recalls Jesus' command to his disciples: "love one another. As I have loved you, so you also should love one another" (John 13:34). The Friday is called Good Friday. Representing the day of Jesus' Crucifixion, it is the most solemn day of the Christian liturgical calendar. The Saturday, referred to as the Easter Vigil, marks the period of anticipation of Jesus' Resurrection. From Thursday through Saturday of the Triduum, the days are marked by major liturgies, as well as morning prayers (called matins) and evening prayers (called vespers). Red and black are often associated with the Triduum.

Easter. This is the high season of celebration in the Christian liturgical calendar because it remembers Jesus' Resurrection. The Easter season begins with Jesus' Sunday Resurrection, celebrates the ascension of Jesus into heaven after his Resurrection, and concludes fifty days after Easter at Pentecost. Pentecost celebrates the descent of the Holy Spirit on Jesus' followers and the birth of the Christian church. The color white usually signifies the Easter season.

Ordinary Time. The second period of Ordinary Time follows Pentecost and lasts for the rest of the year until the start of Advent.

Embedded in the liturgical seasons are the major Christian holidays of Christmas (also called the Nativity) and Easter (also called Pascha). In addition to these holidays, other major observances may occur throughout the year. Among Catholics, for example, highly important observances include celebrations of Mary's Annunciation, when Mary conceived Jesus by the Holy Spirit, on March 25; Mary's Assumption into heaven, when Mary's earthly life ended, on August 15; and All Saints' Day, when the deceased are remembered, on November 1. Others are minor holidays and feast days (for example, days dedicated to certain saints), on which little or no special observance by the community is required.

Sunday is the most common and regular day of Christian worship in the liturgical calendar. Whether a Sunday during a special season or during Ordinary Time, Christians gather in their places of worship to remember, study, and celebrate the life of Jesus. Sunday is the customary day of worship for many Christians because it represents the day of Jesus' Resurrection. Some Christian communities, however, prefer to worship on Saturdays. Such communities frequently align their worship with the Jewish Sabbath, which lasts from sundown on Friday to sundown on Saturday. This practice is maintained in accordance with the Hebraic commandment in the biblical books of Exodus and Deuteronomy to "keep the Sabbath holy" (Exodus 20:8).

The Virgin Mary, Saints, and Martyrs

Throughout Christian history, key figures have surfaced whose extraordinary lives and witness to Christian faith have inspired Christians of later generations. Some of these figures come from the Bible, others from the postbiblical eras, especially the early centuries. In Christian spirituality, only the Trinity (God the Father, God the Son, God the Holy Spirit) is worshipped. However, inspirational figures may become objects of special devotion. A church may be named after a particular figure, for example, who would then be remembered by the congregation in a special way. Certain Christian figures are associated with unique ministries or needs because of things they are believed to have done or incurred in their lives. For example, Saint Peregrine is associated with cancer, reportedly having been cured of cancer himself after a night of prayer, so those with that disease might look to him for inspiration or consolation.

Although Christian figures are not worshipped in a proper sense, some Christian communities believe that persons no longer living are still able to intercede on their behalf. This belief is held because in a Christian worldview, the deceased have not utterly ceased to exist but rather enjoy—or will someday enjoy—ongoing existence with God. Just as Jesus was resurrected, Christians hope for an eschatological, or future, resurrection for themselves. There is, thus, a connection throughout the history of the church, whereby all Christians (deceased, still living, and yet to be born) are in communion with one another. The term for this linkage of Christians across time is the *communion of saints*. In this line of thinking, it makes sense for Christians to feel close to, inspired by, and even aided by remarkable figures from Christian history.

When Christians, and particularly Catholics, feel a special devotion for a particular person, either personally or as a church, they might devote spiritual activities to honoring that person. These may include celebrating the saint's feast day, praying for the intercession of the saint, making a pilgrimage to a historical location of the person, meditating on visual representations of the saint, saying special prayers associated with the saint, doing work or service in the community in accordance with memorable actions of the saint, or naming a child, a church, or an organization after the saint.

Figures for whom Christians may feel special devotion include the Virgin Mary, figures from the Bible, and nonbiblical saints and martyrs.

The Virgin Mary. Jesus' mother, Mary, is particularly important for many Christian communities, especially for Catholic and Orthodox Christians. The New Testament does not provide much information about Mary, and there is comparably little literature about her from the early Christian era. Most of the devotion to Mary, therefore, has developed for theological reasons.

Christians argued, for example, that Mary had special intercessory powers because of her close relationship to Jesus. They also argued that Mary must have been sinless to carry Jesus, who was himself the exemplar of sinlessness, in her womb. Others argued that Mary was actually coresponsible for human salvation, because she bore God Incarnate as Jesus in her womb. At the Council of Ephesus (431), Christian theologians gave Mary the special title of *theotokos* (meaning "God-bearer"). The council, against the Nestorian controversy, concluded that Mary not only bore Jesus as human but Jesus as God. In this sense, it was deemed appropriate to call Mary the Mother of God.

Especially from the fifth century on, Christians found in Mary a special advocate and a feminine element to help balance the often masculine imaging of God in Christianity. Popular devotion to Mary as the Mother of God over the centuries led to the development of two later Marian (related to Mary) doctrines in Roman Catholicism. The first was the 1854 pronouncement by Pope Pius IX of the Immaculate Conception as a dogma of the faith. This doctrine held that Mary was also born sinless, or conceived immaculately. The second, Pius XII's 1950 definition of the Assumption, taught that Mary was assumed into heaven at the end of her life, rather than dying and having her body decay as with ordinary humans.

From the early centuries through the present day, one can find many Marian devotional elements in Christianity. Prayers and hymns, important feast days, and countless private devotions are dedicated to Mary. One of the best-known Marian devotions is the rosary, which is a spoken or silent series of prayers reflecting on the lives of Jesus and Mary, done while holding a string of special beads. Although Mary is not considered a god or part of God, she is seen as the first of the saints and the foremost follower of her son Jesus. Because of the possible error of divinizing Mary, some Christian communities (this was especially true during the Protestant Reformation) eschew devotion to Mary.

Biblical figures. Many biblical figures hold special significance for Christians. Among these are prophets from the Old Testament, such as Jeremiah, Isaiah, and Elijah. Others include angels, such as the archangel Gabriel, who announced to Mary that she would conceive Jesus. Still others are major figures in Jesus' ministry or family life, such as John the Baptist (who baptized Jesus) or Joseph (Mary's husband and Jesus' earthly father).

Some of the most important biblical figures include Jesus' disciples, the first followers of Jesus during his earthly existence. The Gospels of the New Testament record Jesus calling twelve men to be his innermost followers; these are Simon Peter, Andrew, Jude (also called Thaddeus), James of Zebedee, James of Alphaeus, Thomas, Matthew, Phillip, John, Bartholomew, Simon the Zealot, and Judas (to be replaced by Matthias after his betrayal of Jesus). Key figures in the Bible who knew Jesus during his life but are not among the twelve include the women central to Jesus' earthly ministry. They include Mary Magdalene and the two friends of Jesus, Mary and Martha. Finally, apostles are also key biblical figures for Christians. Apostles were the first Christian missionaries. Even though the disciples of Jesus were part of this group, it also included others who spread the good news, such as Paul (the "Apostle to the Gentiles"), who did not know Jesus during Jesus' life.

Christians have special affection for many of these figures. Feast days in the liturgical calendar are dedicated to each of them, and churches and people have been named in their honor. Prayers and practices are associated with them, and particular locations, especially burial places, serve as important sites for Christians to visit.

Saints and martyrs. Between the mid-first century and early fourth century, Christians were a minority population in the Roman Empire. Because of their beliefs, refusal to worship the emperor, and little-known religious practices (after all, they were then a new religious movement), Roman governors sometimes persecuted Christians as scapegoats for political or military defeats and social setbacks. Persecutions under the emperors Nero and Domitian were particularly brutal. Although the number is uncertain, a great many Christians died as "witnesses" (*martyr* means "witness") to their faith during Roman persecutions.

Stories of martyrs' courage and heroism spread far and quickly. Rather than deter people from becoming Christians, these stories inspired people to have courage and faith even in the worst circumstances. Many apostles died as martyrs. Far more martyrs have died in the postbiblical era. Some of these figures, whom Christians also express devotion for, are Ignatius of Antioch, Justin Martyr, Apollonia, Perpetua, and Felicity.

The term *saint* may refer to anyone who has died and is with God (some Christians also consider all living believers to be saints). Christians do not agree on the nature of the state of being that exists between normal human death and the final events of resurrection and judgment. Some view heaven as a present state of being for the deceased; others view it as a future reality. Some view the dead as merely sleeping, awaiting resurrection at the time of Christ's Second Coming; others view the deceased as somehow with God, yet absent the spiritual body they will inherit at the time of resurrection. Christians, moreover, represent a broad spectrum in understanding the scope of salvation (i.e., who is with God or who is or will be in heaven). This ranges from everyone, to only Christians, to only certain Christians. Much of the ambiguity comes from the breadth of possible interpretations of Paul's discussion of resurrection in such passages as 1 Corinthians 15:44b and 15:50–55:

If there is a natural body, there is also a spiritual one. . . .

This I declare, brothers: flesh and blood cannot inherit the kingdom of God, nor does corruption inherit incorruption. Behold, I tell you a mystery. We shall not all fall asleep, but we will all be changed, in an instant, in the blink of an eye, at the last trumpet. For the trumpet will sound, the dead will be raised incorruptible, and we shall be changed. For that which is corruptible must clothe itself with incorruptibility, and that which is mortal must clothe itself with immortality. And when this which is corruptible clothes itself with incorruptibility and this which is mortal clothes itself with immortality. . . . Then the word that is written shall come about.

"Death is swallowed up in victory.
Where, O death, is your victory?
Where, O death, is your sting?"

The Roman Catholic Church has a formal process whereby a person's life may be officially reviewed, and upon meeting certain criteria, the individual is pronounced a saint.

ROMAN CATHOLIC CANONIZATION OF SAINTS

The Roman Catholic Church has a formal process for recognizing a saint. This process is called canonization, because the life of the person is measured (*canon* means a "measuring rod") or assessed for its holiness. The process, which can take hundreds of years to complete, entails several official reviews of the person's life, confirmation of two miracles associated with the deceased figure, and pronouncement of sainthood by the pope. Persons even from modern times are still being canonized as saints.

Pilgrimages. Journeys that Christians make to holy places, places where miracles are believed to occur, or places associated with a Christian saint. Some of the better-known pilgrimage destinations include Jerusalem; Rome; Fatima, Portugal; Lourdes, France; and Guadalupe, Mexico.

Shrines. Sacred spaces within churches, cemeteries, and even homes dedicated to a specific saint. Christians will sometimes visit shrines for special prayer, meditation, and devotion.

Relics. Artifacts believed to come from the deceased bodies or personal possessions of saints. Often shrines or churches will be built in honor of a relic. Because a relic represents a tangible, material connection with a holy person, Christians treat relics with a solemn air of respect and veneration.

Icons. A piece of religious artwork depicting a saint or spiritual event of great significance. Christians sometimes use such artwork as a point of reference for meditation, centering, or prayer. Some Christians treat icons with great respect and even veneration and find meditating or praying with them a vehicle for entering into a deeply religious state of mind.

Social Service and Outreach

Because of their commitment to charity and community, Christians frequently make social service and humanitarian outreach a major part of their spiritual practice. They do this as individuals and families through work and volunteer service. They do this as church communities by running ministries and by engaging in mission activities. Many Christians also see political activism as part of their spirituality.

Christians provide service in countless types of ministries. A short list of Christian ministries includes outreach to the homeless, youth gangs, substance addicts, prison inmates, persons suffering from disease, vulnerable women and children, human trafficking victims, and victims of natural disaster. Ministries also include educational institutions from early childhood through professional preparation, interfaith and peace-making projects, services for orphans, foster care, and adoption, and ecojustice projects.

Christians also engage in missionary activities. Missionary activities are outreach efforts to non-Christians or to people suffering humanitarian crises. Frequently, missionaries have the dual purpose of meeting basic humanitarian needs of a community while also evangelizing the community (or spreading the doctrine of the Christian faith). In past centuries, Christian missionaries were often disrespectful of the native customs and beliefs of peoples they evangelized. Today, however, missionaries generally attempt to respect local culture while simultaneously providing services and education about the Christian faith.

Christians may also be politically active concerning social justice issues about which they feel strongly. There is, of course, no single or correct Christian political platform. Christians appear along the whole political spectrum of liberal to conservative, and Christians of all political persuasions bring their beliefs about morality and justice to the broader public dialogue. Some larger issues that engage Christian political activity include military actions, medical ethics, family legislation, immigration, freedom of speech, freedom of religion, the judicial and penal systems, public education, science and research, and environmental concerns. Often church communities will suggest codes of conduct or guiding principles for their congregations to follow in matters of faith and morality. One example is Catholic social teaching taught by the USCCB, which suggests seven principles of social justice derived from the core belief that every human life is created with inalienable dignity. These principles include respect for the life and dignity of every human person, call to participation in family and community life, human rights and responsibilities, focus on the poor as a gauge of society's adequacy, the right to dignified and fair employment, human solidarity, and care for the environment and the natural world.

Religious Orders

Some Christians, particularly Catholic and Orthodox Christians, choose to live their call to service and justice through membership in a religious community (or congregation). In this context, the term *religious community* refers to an organization of people who adopt, and often make vows to follow, a special way of life oriented around a particular devotional practice, charism, or ministry. A religious community is usually founded or marked by the inspiration of a person who lived a remarkable Christian life and who galvanized others to follow his or her way. For example, a number of religious communities draw their inspiration from Saint Francis of Assisi. There are Protestant, Orthodox, and Catholic religious communities.

In particular, Catholic religious communities have a diverse array of structures, rules, levels of participation, levels of engagement with society at large, and definition of charisms. Some communities are composed of members of the ordained clergy, while others are composed of nonordained persons. Some religious communities are monastic or contemplative and stress minimal or no contact with the outside world, while others are apostolic and stress ministerial service in the world. Some religious communities require all members to take vows of poverty, obedience, and chastity, while others allow members to participate as second- and third-order members (which means they take fewer vows, no vows, or vows for a limited amount of time). When members of religious communities are cloistered (living exclusively within the confines of a monastery), they are called monks and nuns. When members live and work in active ministry outside monasteries, they are called brothers and sisters. Roman

Catholic authorities typically govern religious communities, but each congregation also has its own rules for daily life. Rules govern, for example, the times of day for prayer, mealtimes, and allowable work.

Christian religious communities provide extensive social services throughout the world. In the American context, religious communities (especially women's congregations) historically played a leading role in the health care system and in education from elementary school through college. Religious communities today are often at the cutting edge in meeting social needs and among the first responders to natural disasters and humanitarian crises worldwide.

Conclusion

Christian spirituality refers broadly to how Christians put their faith into practice. Christian spirituality is always rooted in the life of Jesus, and it is generally characterized by the attempt to bring love and service to the whole human community through the special gifts of grace that each Christian individually bears.

Questions for Discussion and Review

1. What does it mean to say Christian spirituality is rooted in the life of Jesus?

2. What do Christians mean by charity?

3. Describe the different types of personal and communal prayer.

4. According to your analysis, which are the three most important aspects of Christian liturgy? Could any be eliminated without compromising the integrity of formal worship?

5. Describe the flow of the liturgical year. Why are some holidays moveable?

6. Name three major categories of historical figures for whom Christians feel special devotion.

7. What sorts of practices, customs, and objects are entailed in special Christian devotions? How do these elements differ from proper worship of God?

8. Give some examples of Christian social service and outreach.
9. What is a religious order? What is the distinction between a nun and a sister, or a monk and a brother?

Key Terms

Advent	Good Friday	Ordinary Time
alb	host/chalice	Palm Sunday
altar	icon	pilgrimage
apostle	lectionary	relic
Ash Wednesday	Lent	religious order
caritas	liturgical year	rites
charism	martyr	rituals
Christocentric	Maundy Thursday	saint
clergy	ministry	theological virtues
disciple	missionary	Triduum
Easter Vigil	Mother of God	vestments

Resources

Holder, Arthur. *Christian Spirituality: The Classics*. New York: Routledge, 2009.

Howard, Evan B. *Brazos Introduction to Christian Spirituality*. Grand Rapids, MI: Brazos, 2008.

McGrath, Alister. *Christian Spirituality: An Introduction*. Malden, MA; Oxford, UK; and Victoria, Australia: Blackwell, 1999.

Tyson, John R. *Invitation to Christian Spirituality: An Ecumenical Anthology*. New York: Oxford University Press, 1999.

7 | Christianity and Non-Christian Religions

CHAPTER

WHAT TO EXPECT

This chapter introduces the relationship between Christian theology and non-Christian religious or spiritual traditions. Christian dialogue with the following belief systems is discussed:

- Judaism
- Islam
- Hinduism and Buddhism

Defining a Religion

Religion in general might be described as a collection of beliefs, held by a community, communicated through symbols, rituals, traditions, and sacred texts, that establishes a worldview and moral code for adherents. This book explores many of these aspects of Christian religion, from its sacred texts and core teachings to spiritual practices and worship communities. The rich diversity within Christianity is emphasized throughout. Still, succinctly describing exactly what the Christian religion is, even after studying it in some depth, is difficult.

All religions, in fact, are difficult to summarize in a few sentences. People of every faith are as varied as Christians. All faith traditions develop diverse expressions, spiritualities, and worship practices over time. People participate in them to varying degrees, from casually to rigorously, from everyday practice to religious vocation or employment. One cannot assume something is true of all Christians, nor can one assume something is true of all members of any religious tradition. Any discussion of religion must be guided by the awareness that a survey can never capture the totality of religious beliefs in lived practice.

Furthermore, people disagree over what actually constitutes a religious tradition. Some define religion as any faith-based belief system to which people commit, as opposed to a belief system based only on observation and experience. Some see belief in God, gods, or a higher power as essential to religion. Still others view religion as culturally derived myths that help believers to explain or make sense of the shared reality that humans struggle to fully understand. More skeptical minds view religions as wishful fantasies born of the desire for justice or fulfillment in the face of socioeconomic or other inequity and the general hardships of life (consider, for example, Sigmund Freud's appraisal of religion in his 1927 book *The Future of an Illusion*).

However one defines *religion*, clearly many worldwide use the term to describe their most essential beliefs and practices. All such adherents must address the fact that multiple religious traditions coexist in the world.

From the beginning of the Christian era, people held sacred multiple religious traditions. Among these traditions were Judaism, the pagan religions of Greece and Rome, and the diverse, competing expressions of Christian faith. Today, as then, Christian theology must carefully and responsibly engage an array of competing or alternative religious worldviews if it is to be attentive to the manifest reality of religious diversity.

Engagement among faith traditions is sometimes difficult. As throughout history, recent decades have witnessed violent conflict among different religious groups (consider the range of contemporary, aggressive religious expressions, from violent cults, to religious terrorism, to "Islamaphobia," to anti-Catholicism). One reason for such conflicts is that religions typically hold ultimate worldviews (or ways people think about and understand the world), and when two or more competing worldviews are present, people can become defensive about their beliefs and feel threatened. However, conflict between religions is rarely *only* theological. Other factors, be they politics, money, land access, and so on, often play a larger role than theology when two groups fight. However, real theological differences often underlie interreligious tension, and looking at these differences can help in understanding and respecting the integrity, beliefs, and humanity of all people. For religious faiths to coexist peacefully and responsibly, religious people need to think carefully about how they interact with other traditions both practically and ideologically.

Christianity and Diversity

Christian theology offers several ways to consider relationships with other religions; three such approaches are exclusive, inclusive, and pluralistic. An exclusivist view would argue that Christianity offers the fullest or best understanding of God's being and relationship to the world. Christian exclusivism rejects the possibility that God's revelation could exist outside the Christian faith and does not see a need for theological dialogue with other faith traditions. This point of view is easy in that it simply does not acknowledge other traditions, but it is functionally inadequate in addressing religious diversity.

An inclusivist view would claim that although Christianity has the fullest understanding of God's being and relationship to the world, God's revelation can also be found outside Christianity. Thus other faith traditions may have insights or practices that could be meaningfully incorporated within Christian faith. This view accommodates other religions but assumes Christianity has a fullness of truth superior to others. Such a belief may inhibit meaningful dialogue between Christian theology and the religions it would engage.

A pluralistic view would contend that no religion is completely adequate for explaining God's being and relationship to the world. All religions can coexist, just as different languages coexist. The existence of Spanish, for example, does not invalidate or compromise the existence of French or German. In a pluralistic model, multiple religions, like multiple languages, may be studied and used to explore and explain the world. The difficulty with this perspective is that it may create an epistemological problem (how to know something is true) in which no religion can be determined as truer or more accurate than another. This situation arises because this approach has no external standards for evaluating or comparing beliefs.

Part of the task of interreligious dialogue is to determine the nature of the dialogue, as well as the expected or desired outcomes. The degree to which people perceive differences among belief systems will largely shape how their dialogue will negotiate those differences. For example, virtually all religions try to make sense of human suffering and loss. In many ways, beliefs among different faith systems are similar regarding essential human experiences, such as birth, marriage, death, and so on. Some maintain that all religions attempt to explain these basic human experiences but each does so using different vocabulary. On the other hand, many argue that differences among religious belief systems are distinct. A polytheistic and a monotheistic conception of the divine, for example, are dramatically different models for thinking about God. As a result, some people hold that religions are trivialized by the effort to equate too quickly their diverse and unique beliefs and practices.

Christians of different worship communions adopt many positions (e.g., exclusive, inclusive, or pluralistic) concerning their own faith in relationship to other belief systems. This chapter discusses pluralist Christian approaches to dialogue from the belief that these are typically the most fruitful and theologically rich.

In considering religious diversity, Christians must negotiate relationships that are both *intra*religious (within Christianity) and *inter*religious (with non-Christian faith traditions). Intrareligious relationships are considered in chapter 5. This chapter surveys Christianity's interreligious relationships with Judaism, Islam, and the Eastern traditions of Hinduism and Buddhism.

Judaism

Christianity is rooted in the same traditions that gave rise to modern Judaism and shares with Judaism the sacred writings of the Hebrew Scriptures (or Tanakh). From the beginning, Christians have affirmed their continuity with the God proclaimed by Israel, the God of Abraham, Isaac, and Jacob. Although historically connected to Judaism, Christianity has not always maintained a peaceful sibling relationship with it. A discussion of Christianity and Judaism requires consideration of historical tensions, as well as present advances in interreligious dialogue.

The principal historical tension between Christianity and Judaism can be summed up by the term *supersessionism*, which refers to

JUDAISM An Overview	LOCATION OF ORIGIN	KEY HISTORICAL FIGURES	FOUNDING DATES
	Mesopotamia and the Fertile Crescent	Abraham, Isaac, Jacob	1800–1300 BCE
SACRED LITERATURE	KEY BELIEFS OR PRACTICES	MAJOR HOLIDAYS	STATUS AND LOCATION TODAY
Tanakh and Talmud	Belief in one God—YHWH Human life was created for covenant with God and observance of the Law; afterlife is undefined Worship at synagogue or temple Worship on Sabbath	Rosh Hashanah (New Year) Yom Kippur (Day of Atonement) Sukkoth (Feast of Booths) Hanukkah (Festival of Lights) Purim (Festival of deliverance from occupation) Passover (Festival commemorating the Exodus) Shavuot (Pentecost)	14 million adherents Worldwide presence, esp. in Israel, Europe, and United States Major sects: Orthodox, Conservative, and Reform

the claim that Christian faith superseded or took the place of the Jewish faith. The majority of the first Christians were themselves Jewish and proclaimed that Jesus fulfilled the ancestral hope for a Messiah. The New Testament holds that Jesus came not to abolish but to fulfill the requirements of Jewish Law (see Matthew 5:17–18). Yet although the earliest Christians continued to follow the Jewish Law, its status as supremely binding was challenged by Jesus' interpretation. The question of how rigorously the Law should be followed factors heavily in New Testament letters. Eventually, as pagan converts to Christianity began to transform the Hebraic character of the early Jesus movement, the practice of the Law was abandoned for exclusively Christian rites and practices.

Even though the Jesus movement was increasingly influenced by Greek culture, Christians continued to claim the Israelite religion as their legacy. Conflict arose over how to understand this legacy, however, as both Christians and Jews claimed it but held different interpretations of its key aspects. The most important conflict concerned the being and nature of the Messiah. For Christians, Jesus was the Messiah; for Jews, the Messiah was to be a political figure expected to deliver the Jewish people from colonial occupation. As the two groups debated, the gap between them grew. Moreover, their debates were not limited to theology; sociopolitical matters were also at issue. For example, in the first Jewish revolt against Roman authorities in 66–70 CE, Christians sought to distance themselves politically from Jews for their own protection as a population within the Roman Empire.

Especially on account of the revolt's failure, of the intensified Roman persecution of Jews, and of the increasingly Hellenistic character of the Jesus movement in the late first century, many Christians saw Christianity as having superseded Judaism, as having fulfilled its commandments and replaced Jewish Law with worship of Jesus. This claim, compounded by the misguided notion that Jews were responsible for Jesus' death (in fact, only Roman governors could inflict capital punishment at the time), led later generations of Christians to often-coercive and violent treatment of Jewish people.

Anti-Semitism is a term used to describe violent actions and attitudes toward Jews. Anti-Semitism continues today. Some of its most brutal historical expressions include the Catholic Inquisitions in the Middle Ages and the German Holocaust (also known as the Shoah) in the twentieth century. Responsible Christian theology today attempts to redress anti-Semitism by rejecting claims that Christianity supersedes Judaism, rejecting claims that Jews were responsible for Jesus' death, and seeking out, naming, and rejecting anti-Semitic attitudes and actions, whether past or present expressions.

Today Christian and Jewish scholars and religious leaders recognize the benefits of engaging in genuine theological dialogue. In recent decades, Christian theologians have renewed their interest in the persistent and pervasive threads of Hebraic thought and culture in Christian scriptural tradition. Members of both religions recognize that engaging one another, even in debate, is a valid expression of vital and dynamic faith. The biblical tradition each shares is not one of easy answers but rather one of searching, questioning, and even challenging God. The practice of vigorous dialogue with God is increasingly seen as essential in both Christian and Jewish faith. Fruitful areas for Christian–Jewish dialogue include the Jewishness of Jesus, the Hebrew Scriptures, nonsupersessionism, and eschatological hopes and tensions.

Jesus: A Jewish man. Focusing on the Jewish character and heritage of Jesus is important for Christians interested in the roots of Christianity. Christian doctrine that too quickly focuses on advanced Christological concerns and terms may overlook the need to ground Christ in the historical person of Jesus. Appreciation of the Hebraic context in which Jesus emerged, especially the prophetic tradition he embodied, may move Christians toward richer dialogue with Jews.

The Hebrew Scriptures. Historically, Christians have erred in reading the Hebrew literature as if it were exclusively oriented toward the foretelling of Jesus' life and death. Excessive emphasis on the Christocentric nature of Hebrew prophecy can interfere with a rich reading of the Hebrew Scriptures as an inherently integrated and meaningful set of texts. Although, in the Hebrew literature, Christians may see continuity with the Christ events, Christian theologians advance interreligious dialogue with Judaism by developing skill in reading the texts apart from a rigid Christocentric interpretation.

Nonsupersessionism. Christian theologians aid interreligious dialogue with Judaism by articulating alternatives to supersessionist theology. This involves a renewed understanding of both Christian conceptions of God's covenant through Jesus and Jewish conceptions of God's covenant through the Law.

Eschatological hopes and tensions. Christianity and Judaism may also share political interests, driven by overlapping eschatological perspectives. Christians often speak in the language of hope for the return of Christ, although they differ considerably on what precisely they hope or believe will happen. Jews often speak in the language of hope for the restoration of the Temple in Jerusalem, although this hope varies widely among different Jewish groups. Some Christians believe that rebuilding the Jerusalem Temple will usher in the era of Christ's return to earth. Rebuilding the Temple on the Temple

Mount in Jerusalem, where two Muslim mosques currently sit, however, would have global political ramifications. The politicization and political consequences of faith can produce extreme social tension. As Jews, Christians, and Muslims attempt to negotiate the volatile realities of life in the Middle East, especially in the State of Israel, subscribers to all faiths are tasked with engaging responsibly and genuinely to achieve peaceful coexistence.

Islam

Like Christianity and Judaism, Islam claims Abraham as its founding father. Whereas Christians and Jews establish their lineage through Abraham's son Isaac, Muslims trace their lineage through Abraham's other son, Ishmael. Islam teaches that Abraham, with the help of Ishmael, built the Kaaba, the most sacred building in the Islamic tradition. The lineage to Abraham that all three traditions trace places them in a sibling relationship with one another. Beyond Abraham, all three religions share a concept of God as the monotheistic deity revealed by the prophets of Israel. All three have a vested interest in sacred locations throughout Palestine. All three share overlapping accounts of revelation in Scripture and the information contained therein concerning God's relationship to humanity.

Probably because of the similarity of these religions, their historical relationships have been tense and often violent. Any discussion of the dialogue among them, specifically the bilateral dialogue between Christians and Muslims, must recognize the tensions that have long constituted their theological and sociopolitical conflicts (for example, the Crusades of the Middle Ages, as well as contemporary Mideast religiopolitical conflicts, especially surrounding the State of Israel, that have intermittently resulted in terrorism and war throughout the twentieth and twenty-first centuries). Today these conflicts are seen in renewed expressions of terror and war, making a committed effort at interreligious dialogue between Christians and Muslims all the more urgent.

The major theological differences between Christianity and Islam may be folded into the following key categories: the understanding of God, the prophet Muhammad, revelation in the Qur'an, and engagement with the world.

ISLAM An Overview	LOCATION OF ORIGIN	KEY HISTORICAL FIGURES	FOUNDING DATE
	Mecca in Saudi Arabia	Muhammad	622 CE

SACRED LITERATURE	KEY BELIEFS OR PRACTICES	MAJOR HOLIDAYS	STATUS AND LOCATION TODAY
Qur'an Sunnah and Hadith collections	Belief in one God—Allah Goal for life is submission to God in the hope of resurrection after death and paradise after the Day of Judgment Worship in mosque Observance of the Five Pillars of Islam: 1. Profession of the creed (shahadah) 2. Recitation of daily prayers (salat) 3. Almsgiving (zakah) 4. Fasting during Ramadan 5. Pilgrimage to Mecca (Hajj)	Muharram (New Year) Ashura (Day of mourning) Mawlid al-Nabi (Muhammad's birthday) Ramadan (month of fasting) Eid al-Fitr (celebration ending the fasting of Ramadan) Eid al-Adha (celebration ending the Hajj)	1.5 billion adherents Worldwide presence, esp. in Middle East, Africa, North America, and Europe Major sects: Sunni, Shia, Sufi

Understanding of God. Islam and Christianity both assert belief in the monotheistic God. Indeed, the same God professed in the biblical tradition of Israel is recognized by both religions as One and True. Islam derives from the same tradition that produced Judaism and Christianity but sees itself as the completion of and correction to its predecessors.

Islam's chief dispute with the Christian understanding of God lies in the latter's Trinitarian and Christological claims. For Christians, God interacts with humanity in a personal way, expressed through the persons of the Trinity and the Incarnation of Christ. Christians identify Jesus as part of or one with the One God and who also thus brings salvation in an immediate, direct, and personal encounter between God and humanity. For Muslims, God's oneness is utterly transcendent, and human claims to personal intimacy with God are judged to be presumptuous, even dangerous. In Islam, God's will is revealed not through a personal incarnation but through the succession of prophets begun in the Old Testament and concluded in the final revelation of the prophet Muhammad. Both groups may err in oversimplifying or exaggerating the claims of the other regarding, respectively, the Islamic insistence on God's transcendence and the Christian insistence on God's personal encounter.

The prophet Muhammad. As noted earlier, Christianity historically struggled against Judaism because of its claims to supersede Jewish Law and covenant. In the case of Judaism, Christianity has had to reenvision its relationship to its older sibling. With Islam, Christianity must reenvision its relationship with its younger sibling.

The prophet Muhammad was born in Mecca in 570 CE and died in 632. According to Muslim belief, nearly six hundred years after the life of Jesus, the prophet received the revelation. This revelation, along with the life and deeds of the prophet as recorded in the Sunnah, provides the basis for Islamic practice and belief. Given to Muhammad in the last twenty-three years of his life, the revelation was recorded scrupulously in the Book of God, known as the Qur'an.

Muslims do not see Muhammad as the incarnation of God, as Christians see Jesus. Rather, Islam teaches that Muhammad is God's final prophet, who fulfills the revelation begun with Abraham and carried through the biblical traditions and the life of Jesus. Muhammad's prophetic revelation teaches about God's purpose in creating and commands humans to live ethical lives, create just communities, and submit rightfully to God. Although Muhammad is not worshipped as a deity, Muslims consider his role to be inestimable because he transmits God's revelation, to which humans would otherwise have no access.

Christianity has not historically recognized Muhammad as a prophet, let alone as God's final and fullest prophet. This represents one of the greatest theological tensions between the two religions. Perhaps Christians have traditionally rejected Muhammad because Islam postdates the events of Christ. Even more likely, they have done so because of Christianity's unique claims about the salvation experience in Jesus, which renders the role of all prophets secondary to the Christ event. Some also suggest that Christians have rejected the prophet Muhammad because of the hostile conditions in which early Islam spread under the prophet. Whatever the explanation, Christian theologians engaged in Islamic interreligious dialogue now take seriously the claim that Muhammad is a prophet and attempt (with varying levels of success) to understand him meaningfully in the tradition of the biblical prophets such as Isaiah and Jeremiah (see, for example, the work of Hans Küng).

Revelation in the Qur'an. Islam teaches that God's revelation was fully and perfectly made to the prophet Muhammad and recorded in the Arabic text of the Qur'an. For Islam, this book represents the very Word of God. Its sacred character to Muslims cannot be overstated, and because of the unique nature of the Qur'an, it cannot, according to Muslims, be treated the same as other written texts. For example, it cannot be properly translated. Although translations are made, the Arabic text remains the most perfect and definitive expression of the revelation. In addition, while the Qur'an is to be studied, it is not subject to historical or developmental analysis as other writings might be.

Like Muslims, Christians claim that their sacred revelation, the Bible, is the Word of God. Also as Muslims say of the Qur'an, many Christians claim that the Bible is an inerrant, sacred revelation. However, in the last two centuries, many Christian communions have adopted methods of biblical scholarship that allow them to see the Bible as human-authored but divinely inspired, a compilation of writings produced over several centuries and reflecting different time periods, and redacted (or edited) to reflect worldviews pertinent to a range of sociopolitical contexts throughout that history.

Although not all Christians embrace the notion of historical-critical study of the Bible, it is the reigning model of scholarly analysis and is broadly persuasive for millions of Christians. By contrast, historical-critical analysis of the Qur'an militates against the very notion of the unique and total revelation made to Muhammad. As such, Christians and Muslims dispute the value and appropriateness of bringing such analytic techniques to Qur'anic study. The high-stakes questions of how to read sacred literature, including the Bible and the Qur'an, and the level of interpretive criticism one should bring to it, remain important areas for discussion (and sometimes areas of conflict) between Christians and Muslims.

Engagement with the world. Both Christianity and Islam are missionizing religions, meaning they seek to bring their message and beliefs to persons all over the world. One can imagine that the targets of this missionizing work may not always welcome such efforts. Muslims and Christians might well see each other as groups that need to be missionized or converted. This attitude of mission toward the world has historically been a keen source of tension, sometimes leading to feelings of oppression and subsequent expressions of violence.

Mission practice today, most would argue, needs to be mindful of the integrity of all people and to pursue a noncoercive and politically neutral course if it is to be tolerated and socially constructive. Related to this are ethical questions that straddle civil and religious laws in societies where Muslims and Christians coexist; one current area rife with such ethical questions is that of women's social roles and rights. The missionary and sociopolitical expressions of the Muslim and Christian faiths invite both faiths to advance and develop their dialogue in the current era.

These aspects of theological difference constitute the framework for modern Christian–Muslim dialogue. The style Christians use in this dialogue, and the success they achieve, varies tremendously. As noted, there are many Christian voices, and all do not regard interreligious dialogue with the same level of concern nor approach it with the same level of nuance or skill. Recalling the categories of exclusivist, inclusivist, and pluralistic views is useful, as they suggest the possible directions this dialogue may take. Christian and Muslim mutual exclusivism is problematic insofar as it negates genuine and constructive dialogue. Christian and Muslim inclusivist approaches may be more constructive. However, the inclusivist approach risks mutual appropriating, diminishing, distorting, or subverting of each other's original and essential claims, leading to a false or superficial sense of agreement. Perhaps the best approach to Christian–Muslim dialogue would be pluralistic, wherein both partners try first and foremost to enter into the religious beliefs of the other—first to understand as a native believer would and then to analyze as a point of comparison. The most successful Christian theological attempts to dialogue seriously with Islam to date have taken a pluralistic approach.

HOLY WAR?

War is not principally played out theologically. It occurs in the realm of the polis, conducted by soldiers or citizens, and its outcomes affect politics, economics, geographical boundaries, and so on. What does religion have to do with war? One aspect of modern-day interreligious conflict that garners great popular attention is the idea of holy war. Immediately, upon even considering the term *holy war*, many people are inclined to ask, How can war be holy? How can God, or the gods, of any religion justify or mandate the violence of war?

It is sometimes surprising to discover that the history of religions is integrally related to political history and therefore to war. This is because religion does not exist in a vacuum in the hearts and minds of believers; it exists as the operating worldview that fundamentally drives and motivates people who are inescapably immersed in their social contexts. Religious justifications for war can be offered for any number of reasons. Such reasons include that:

- the sacred texts of the religion speak of, mandate, or justify war, as happens in the sacred books of Judaism, Christianity, and Islam
- religious leaders call believers to war, as happened in the Crusades or in modern-day religious terrorism
- people believe God has called them as "soldiers" to enforce a certain moral code or social ethos, as happens in contemporary, religiously motivated abortion clinic bombings
- people feel God wants them to reclaim sacred territory or spaces of historical import to the religion, as occurs in the contemporary Hindu-Muslim clashes in Kashmir, India

Continued

Continued

- people of two or more different religions or sects within a religion vie for the same land or resources, each believing that God is on their side and opposed to the other
- people feel God wants them to go to war to stop an injustice or to liberate a people from oppression

Among the more important present-day considerations of holy war is that of Islamic jihad. The term *jihad* means "struggle," and it is a religious duty of Muslims. This struggle is often misinterpreted by non-Muslims as referring exclusively to the struggle of holy warfare. In fact, *jihad* refers more broadly to the multifaceted Islamic struggle to maintain one's faith, to live in rightful submission to God, to improve the conditions of society, and to defend the Islamic faith. Islam accordingly speaks of jihad of the heart, jihad of the tongue, and jihad of the hand, as well as jihad of the sword.

Like Islam, Christianity has a long tradition of thinking about holy war. As soon as Christianity became the leading religion of the Roman Empire in the fourth century, Christian theologians such as Saint Augustine were tasked to consider what conditions merited force in the interests of the empire. "Just war theory" emerged with arguments from Augustine and Thomas Aquinas that force could be used when certain conditions were met, including when war was initiated by a proper authority, was conducted for a just cause, was conducted by ethical means, had a chance for victory in combat, and was motivated by right intent.

The Crusades of the Middle Ages exemplify the terrible violence that can come from holy war rationale. Even a superficial study of the Crusades reveals that much more than religious debate was at stake among combating Eastern Christians, Western Christians, Muslims, and Jews. This dangerous historical epic is a useful talking point for comparison when one evaluates all modern-day warfare that is justified or invoked subtly or overtly by religious claims or religious leaders. In considering modern war it is also helpful to ask, Under what conditions is war just? What elements in religions justify or even mandate the use of violence?

Christianity and Two Eastern Traditions

Christianity's dialogue partners extend beyond Judaism and Islam. Any cultural context wherein Christianity exists provides a possible location for interreligious dialogue. All such dialogues are interesting and valuable dimensions of theological study. In the interest of brevity alone, this chapter cannot consider all of Christianity's dialogue partners. Some of these include Sikhism, Jainism, the Baha'i faith, Taoism, Confucianism, modern forms of paganism, Wicca, and Scientology, as well as Native American, African, and other indigenous religions. Christian dialogue with many of these groups involves the broader issue of Christian missiology, or the study of how and why Christians bring their message to non-Christians.

This section discusses two key Eastern religious traditions that Christians encounter: Hinduism and Buddhism. These religions, perhaps better thought of as spiritual traditions, are sometimes lumped together as "Eastern religions" but in fact are distinct systems that warrant individual attention.

Hinduism

Christianity and Hinduism have widely differing accounts of revelation, theological anthropology, salvation, and afterlife. One can see these differences clearly by examining how each understands the nature and purpose of the human person. For Christians, human beings were made in the image of God but in their free will succumbed to sin. This resulted in a fall from grace and a need for salvation. Jesus uniquely offers salvation and restores his followers to a state of grace. At the end of life, human beings await resurrection and heavenly existence.

By contrast, Hinduism holds that each human being carries the spark of the divine within. However, humans have forgotten their true nature and need to recall it. Human life is understood as a series of incarnations that leads ultimately to realization of one's true nature and liberation from the cycles of incarnation. The Advaita school of thought in Hinduism is "nondualistic" and holds that the self is liberated when it realizes itself as in no way separated or essentially distinct from the ultimate reality of Brahman. The Dvaita school

HINDUISM An Overview	LOCATION OF ORIGIN	KEY HISTORICAL FIGURES	FOUNDING DATE
	India	No specific founder	1500 BCE
SACRED LITERATURE	KEY BELIEFS OR PRACTICES	MAJOR HOLIDAYS	STATUS & LOCATION TODAY

• Vedas
• Upanishads
• Sutras
• Puranas
• Epics:
  Bhagavad Gita,
  Ramayana,
  Mahabharata
	Brahman is the ultimate reality
	
	Goal for life is to attain liberation from the cycle of reincarnation through following the dharma and understanding the nature of the self
	
	Worship in temples or domestic shrines
		Diwali (Festival of Lights)
		
		Holi (Festival of Colors)
		
		Festivals of deities' birthdays and seasonal festivals
			900 million adherents
			
			Worldwide presence, esp. India, United Kingdom, United States
			
			Major sects: Saivism, Vaisnavism, Saktism, Smartism

of thought holds opposingly that souls are eternal and retain their distinctness within the ultimate reality of Brahman.

Despite significant theological differences between Christianity and Hinduism, these religions invite constructive dialogue among contemporary theologians. For example, the Hindu conception of God, like the Christian one, may be helpfully understood in Trinitarian language. Hinduism conceives of God as manifesting in the three principal aspects of Brahma, Vishnu, and Shiva, which may be compared with the Trinitarian Christian categories of Father, Son, and Spirit. In addition, the Hindu concept of liberation (called *moksha*) from the cycle of reincarnation (called *samsara*) may also be compared with the Christian concept of liberation from sin and eschatological salvation. Hindu and Christian spiritual and contemplative practices, such as yoga and meditation, may also be explored and compared. Both traditions contemplate the Divine Being and the Divine Presence in human beings, suggesting the possibility of interior illumination, divine intercession in human affairs, and revelatory insight. Hindus and Christians share a relatively peaceful history, but Christian missionizing in India has sometimes led to violence and political conflict.

Westerners have become increasingly aware of Hinduism, especially as an alternative to traditional conceptions of "church" and an enriching option for spiritual practice and development. The Hindu-Christian dialogue is producing a growing body of comparative theological study aimed at sharing information, mutual understanding, and collaboration.

Buddhism

Many Westerners are attracted to the spiritual, meditative practices of Buddhism. As with Hinduism, Christianity has increasingly engaged Buddhism in recent times. The Buddhist–Christian dialogue has become so sophisticated as to produce professional journals, partnerships, and academic centers of study.

As with any religious tradition, a good way of approaching Buddhism is to grasp its understanding of human life. A central tenet of Buddhism is the idea that human life, indeed all life, is transitory. Although people perceive themselves and others as distinct individuals, Buddhism teaches that people do not have fixed, eternal souls. This is the idea of *an-atman*, or no-soul, in Buddhism. Suffering marks human experience because people misunderstand the basic fluidity of all nature and try to attach themselves permanently to that which is impermanent. This is especially true of human attachment to one's life, one's material goods, and one's relationships with others. Liberation from suffering comes in the form of enlightenment about the true nature of reality. Lifestyle and meditative practice, guided by the Buddha's teachings of the Four Noble Truths and Eightfold Path, can help Buddhists achieve enlightenment and freedom from suffering and to live joyfully and compassionately to help eliminate suffering in the world.

There is significant overlap between Buddhism and Christianity on the issue of human suffering and how that suffering may be overcome. Moreover, Buddhism and Christianity have a central, liberating, historical figure: the Buddha and Jesus, respectively. Both traditions study the lives of the key historical figures at their origins, providing fruitful opportunities for comparison. Both traditions also teach faith-based practices aimed at compassion and liberation from suffering. Christian–Buddhist dialogue that focuses on doctrine,

BUDDHISM An Overview	LOCATION OF ORIGIN	KEY HISTORICAL FIGURES	FOUNDING DATE
	India	Siddhartha Gautama (also called the Buddha)	520 BCE

SACRED LITERATURE	KEY BELIEFS OR PRACTICES	MAJOR HOLIDAYS	STATUS AND LOCATION TODAY
Pali Canon	Everything is impermanent Attainment of enlightenment (Nirvana) through observance of the Four Noble Truths: 1. All life is suffering. 2. Suffering is caused by desire. 3. Suffering can be eliminated . . . 4 . . . by following the Noble Eightfold Path: • right view • right intention • right speech • right conduct • right livelihood • right effort • right mindfulness • right concentration Meditation in a temple	The Buddha's birthday The Buddha's Enlightenment	360 million Worldwide presence, esp. in Japan, China, Korea, and Asia Major sects: Theravada, Mahayana, Vajrayana

therefore, may consider categories of suffering, ethical and meditative teachings, selfhood, no-selfhood, and divine illumination.

An interesting aspect of Buddhist teachings is that they are often expressed in negative terms. This means that Buddhist teaching inclines more toward telling what something is *not* like than by asserting what it *is* like. In Christian theology, there is a comparable tradition called the *via negativa* (the way of the negative), whereby God is contemplated by negative analogies; for example, "God is not limited," "God is not alterable," and so on. Buddhism does not assert specific dogmas about the interior life or being of the Divine (as do the Christian doctrines of Trinity or Incarnation). Thus Christian theologians have been particularly open to Buddhist teaching insofar as they have been able to assume an inclusivist approach, incorporating aspects of Buddhist spirituality into a Christian framework without having to accommodate competing assertions about God.

In addition to doctrinal comparisons, Christian and Buddhist dialogue mutually engage questions of social ethics and personal conduct. Both traditions recognize the reality of suffering and seek to alleviate it through a compassionate, human response. Moreover, both see that human response as the result of transcendent insight. Both further stress the need for right personal conduct and prescribe meditative practices aimed at developing a mature spirituality. Thus Christian–Buddhist dialogue can mutually enrich each religion's sense of social participation and personal spirituality as a corrective response to suffering.

Conclusion

Christian faith is but one of many faith traditions in the world. The reality of multiple religious traditions calls on Christians to think constructively and dialogically about their relationship to others. The potential for misunderstanding, conflict, and even violence is too great to ignore.

The discussion of the potential directions for Christian inter-religious dialogue has considered its sibling traditions and traditions further removed theologically, geographically, and historically. The closest traditions to Christianity are Judaism and Islam. These religions stem from the same historical lineage and share closely overlapping themes in their sacred literatures and doctrines of God. It is also with these religions that Christianity has had the most historical conflict. Negotiating present-day political tensions requires an elevated care and commitment to interreligious dialogue among these faiths.

The Eastern faiths of Hinduism and Buddhism also constitute important dialogue partners for Christians. These dialogues have increasing relevance today as Hinduism and Buddhism more broadly permeate the spiritual practice and popular imagination of people in the West. Christian interreligious dialogues with traditions not mentioned in this chapter are extensive and also involve the study of Christian missionary practices.

There are, finally, many different Christian communities, each with its own understanding of the purpose of interreligious dialogue. For some, such dialogue is unnecessary and unwanted. For others, it is the most burning issue the community faces. Christians may adopt any number of attitudes toward interreligious dialogue. Typically, those attitudes are either exclusive, inclusive, or pluralistic. Each approach has theological strengths and drawbacks, but the inclusive and pluralist approaches tend to produce the best outcomes for continued mutual theological engagement.

Questions for Discussion and Review

1. What is the difference between interreligious and intrareligious dialogue?
2. Distinguish among inclusive, exclusive, and pluralistic approaches to interreligious dialogue.
3. Why are Judaism, Christianity, and Islam considered "Abrahamic faiths"?
4. Name several non-Christian religions with which Christianity might dialogue.
5. What are the principal areas of dialogue between Christian and Jewish thought?
6. What are the principal areas of dialogue between Christian and Islamic thought?
7. What are some theological similarities and differences between Hindu and Christian thought?
8. What are some theological similarities and differences between Buddhist and Christian thought?

9. Is interreligious dialogue necessary in the world today? Explain.

10. How would you respond to the statement, "Christians don't need to dialogue with that group because they only espouse a philosophy, not a religion."

Key Terms

an–atman	Ishmael	Qur'an
anti-Semitism	Kaaba	*samsara*
the Buddha	missiology	Shoah
Eastern religions	*moksha*	Sunnah
enlightenment	nonsupersessionism	supersessionism
exclusivist approach	pluralistic approach	ultimate worldviews
inclusivist approach	prophet Muhammad	

Resources

Chittister, Joan, Murshid Shaadi Shakur Chisti, and Arthur Waskow. *The Tent of Abraham: Stories of Hope and Peace for Jews, Christians, and Muslims.* Boston: Beacon, 2006.

Ford, David F., and Rachel Muers, eds. *Theology between Faiths, pt. VII,* in *The Modern Theologians: An Introduction to Christian Theology since 1918.* 3rd ed. Oxford, UK: Blackwell, 2005.

Küng, Hans, Josef von Ess, Heinrich von Steitencron, and Heinz Bechert. *Christianity and World Religions: Paths of Dialogue with Islam, Hinduism, and Buddhism.* Maryknoll, NY: Orbis, 1999.

Robert, Dana L. *Christian Mission: How Christianity Became a World Religion.* Oxford, UK: Wiley-Blackwell, 2009.

Smith, Huston. *The World's Religions.* New York: HarperOne, 2009.

Smock, David R., ed. *Interfaith Dialogue and Peacebuilding.* Washington, DC: U.S. Institute of Peace Press, 2002.

8 | Christianity and the World
CHAPTER

WHAT TO EXPECT

This chapter examines Christianity and its relationship to the secular world. Three major aspects of that relationship are considered:

- Christianity and science
- Christianity and politics
- justice and ethics

Christianity and the Secular World

Christianity entails many things: ideas, people, practices, literature, traditions, and so on. All the elements that the Christian religion comprises exist *in the world*. It might be tempting to think of religion as somehow separate or different from the world because it points to transcendent realities and ideas. Even though religion may point beyond the natural world, however, everything that human beings do—including things religious—must occur in the world. This inevitable worldliness is a fact of human existence, which raises questions about how Christian thought and practice should be lived out in concrete ways. In its entirety, Christian thought establishes a worldview that systematically attempts to account for both epistemology (what can be known) and morality (what ought to be done and how). These areas necessarily intersect with the world at large.

Sometimes a Christian worldview and a secular one meet harmoniously. For example, both secular culture and Christian thought can support ecological conservationism. A secular reason to support conservationism might be that ecologically-based practices bolster a local economy, while a Christian reason to support it might be that all of God's creation should be stewarded responsibly. These two justifications for conservationism, although essentially different, complement each other.

Sometimes, however, a Christian and a secular worldview might conflict in a way that is dissonant or even intolerable. For example, corporate interests often run contrary to more environmentally sound business practices. A Christian ethic of environmental stewardship may be neglected or disregarded in favor of a company's focus on profit. Medical issues are another area of conflict. Christian ethics, emphasizing individual human dignity and worth, the value of life at all stages of development, and the importance of a broad understanding of human flourishing, can clash with positions that emphasize values of convenience, or absolute optimization of individual material and physical well-being. The outcome is conflict in the lives and practices of Christians navigating health care issues in the real world, as both consumers and health care providers. Moreover, in both examples, there can be any number of complications: What say or voting power do Christians actually have in shaping business or medical practices? How much should a Christian perspective steer laws guiding these practices? Which position will win when the so-called Christian perspective on a question of medical or business ethics is disputed internally among Christians? And so on.

As already considered, Christians are required to negotiate plurality among themselves, as well as with people of other religions. A perhaps more encompassing task than either of these, however, is that Christians are challenged to engage the world itself. In so doing, Christians must ask questions such as, How should Christians think about the discoveries of modern science, especially when they appear to run contrary to established Christian doctrine? How are Christians to respond to claims that religion is an outmoded and even dangerous way of thinking? How and to what degree should Christians publicly voice their opinions in legislation? How should

Christians resolve internal disputes on gay marriage, abortion, evolution, health care coverage, and other contentious matters? In both harmonious and contentious situations, Christians face the challenge of living out their beliefs in meaningful ways in daily practice. This includes every aspect of life—from where Christians work, to where they invest their money, to where they shop, to how they vote, and so forth.

This chapter considers just three categories of Christian engagement and dialogue with the world: science, politics, and justice. As with previous discussions, it is important to note that this brief survey in no way exhausts the many possibilities for Christian engagement or the diverse worldviews various Christian people and communions bring to each of these forums.

Christianity and Science

From the beginning of the Christian era, Christian thinkers have recognized that faith and reason complement each other. Although occasionally in Christian thought, purely fideistic (faith-based) expressions of belief trump rational (reason-based) approaches, the overwhelming consensus in Christianity is that people are encouraged to use reason to explore and understand the world. Christian thinkers—from the earliest writers to contemporary theologians—have looked to a reason-based understanding of the world to enhance their knowledge of God.

Using reason to complement faith rests on two underlying tenets of a Christian worldview. The first tenet is that God created freely. The belief that God created the world suggests the world is a place where people can come to know God. In other words, the world is not random, mechanical, or arbitrary, but rather the intentioned and loving work of a free Creator. As such, the world is like an artist's canvas or a school where God's character reveals itself. Reason is rightly employed to study the world, because studying the world is an aspect of studying God. A corollary to this belief is that outcomes of reason-based inquiry may be surprising or reveal something new about the world. The world is not "given" or utterly predictable but is a place of discovery. Moreover, human reason itself is a component of God's creation. Christians have seen reason as God's highest blessing and gift to the human species. Indeed, reason is in part what makes humans bearers of the image of God, and Christians therefore find it fitting to use their reason in relationship to the world.

The second tenet is that God created human beings to be free. Human freedom acts in dialogue with the freedom by which God created the world. When something is free, its outcome is not pre-ordained. It is not bound by necessity or obligation but is open to new possibilities, new discoveries, and new developments. The whole basis of scientific investigation, invention, human technology, and so on presumes a fundamental freedom. Using freedom to engage the world creatively is a unique vocation of the human species, one that requires the full exercise of reason.

If reason and faith complement each other, then one might ask why there seems to be such tension between Christianity and science today. An exploration of several points of contention proves neces-sary here. These include biblical interpretation, evolutionary theory, and the definition of the term *science*.

Biblical Interpretation

As already discussed, people can meaningfully read the Bible in many different ways: for inspiration, for consolation, for knowledge of God, for wisdom, and so on. However, reading the Bible well requires an understanding of the nature of the texts. Just as one would be disappointed if one looked to the phone book for poetic inspiration or to a comic book for directions on installing a new dishwasher, so too is it possible for people to become frustrated if they read the Bible without understanding the nature of what they are reading.

Trying to read the Bible as if it provides a natural history of the world is a common mistake. In particular, people make this error when reading the books of the Old Testament, especially the Creation stories in Genesis. Though some books of the Bible do offer a geopolitical history of the kingdoms of Judah and Israel, the Old Testament mostly relates the story of the covenant relationship between the people of Israel and God. This love story is told in fables, poems, liturgies, songs, and myths. Even the historical aspects are told and retold in various lights, depending on what was happening at the time of their final recording.

If one were to consider what the human writers of the Bible thought they were recording, one could come up with many possibilities, but "a natural history of the earth" would not likely be one of them. The concept of natural history, based on sciences such as archaeology and paleontology, would have been unknown to the writers of the Bible. But if not to provide a natural history, then how might the Creation stories, for example, function in the Bible? Biblical writings on the origins of life do two things: they attribute the totality of life and the cosmos to the work of a single, powerful Creator, and they retain an awe and mystery about the Creator's work, suggesting that human beings have a restricted capacity to understand it. In other words, the Creation stories affirm God as the Creator and call human beings to recognize their humility before the Creator. The Creation stories in Genesis are complemented in the book of Job and its depiction of God's incomprehensible mastery over nature. Among the most profound insights of this text is that human knowledge is insufficient to grasp the full power and mystery of God. Thus these biblical stories use the language of poetry and myth, literary forms well suited to communicate the inexplicable.

Early Christian interpreters of the Bible did not have a problem recognizing poetry and myth; they felt no need to interpret these stories as a natural history of the earth in order to appreciate their truth. They recognized that providing spiritual illumination far outweighs historical accuracy as the intent of the biblical writers. Tensions or contradictions in the text were seen as opportunities to delve further into the layers of revelation and as invitations to find truth beyond the superficial accounts of past events.

So when did people begin reading the Bible as a source for natural history? Conversely, when did many Christians lose the ability to read the Bible as poetry, with humor, and as fables with a moral point? Answering these questions requires an exploration into modern science and the theory of evolution.

CONTEMPORARY DEBATE ABOUT NATURAL THEOLOGY

Natural theology is the branch of theology that tries to demonstrate through reason alone the existence of God, as well as the divine purpose and design of creation. Natural theology therefore does not rely on revelation to prove God but rather asserts that God can be known through the study of the natural world itself. From the time of the Greek philosophers and the beginning of the Christian era, people have attempted to know the divine purpose of the world through rational inquiry. The endeavor to know God apart from special revelation became a special point of interest during the Enlightenment of the seventeenth and eighteenth centuries, characterized by the turn toward reason. In 1802 the English theologian and moral philosopher William Paley published a work called *Natural Theology*, representing a classic distillation of the rational attempt to prove God.

Rational arguments for the existence of God and the purpose and design of nature have met with mixed success historically. Anselm of Canterbury (1033–1109) argued that "God is that, more than which cannot be conceived," and Thomas Aquinas argued that there were "five ways" (motion, causation, contingency/necessity, degree/perfection, and intelligent design) in which God was implied in the fabric of creation itself. Such arguments have been countered by critics like David Hume (1711–1776), who argued that nature does not prove inherent purpose or design and that deriving God from nature is speculative rather than conclusive.

In recent decades the natural theology dialogue has experienced renewed interest by a panoply of scientists and theologians. Physicist and Church of England clergyman John Polkinghorne (b. 1930), for example, has argued for the complementarity of theology and physics. His work represents the contemporary trend in natural theology, which argues that theological and scientific

Continued

Continued

models together provide a fuller and more coherent explanation of the natural world than either would independently. Conversely, staunch critics of natural theology, such as Richard Dawkins (b. 1941), look at the same evidence and conclude that God either does not exist or cannot be proven. As scientists continue to penetrate ever deeper into the universe's mysteries, the debate over whether God can be demonstrated or not, apart from revelation, will only intensify.

Evolutionary Theory

Imagine that today you learned you had inherited $10 million. That knowledge would change your sense of everything. The same thing happens as major new discoveries about the universe reframe how it is understood. The discovery that Earth revolved around the sun was one such moment. Before Galileo confirmed the Copernican heliocentric theory of the solar system in the seventeenth century, people believed the sun revolved around Earth. Because many people believed humans to be the greatest creatures on Earth, it followed that these people believed humans to be literally the center of the universe. The discovery that Earth is only one of many planets that revolve around the sun seemed to diminish this sense of human importance. Such an alteration in thinking is called a paradigm shift, which, although both immediate and dramatic, can take decades or centuries to be fully accepted.

In 1859 Charles Darwin published the book *On the Origin of Species*, in which he theorized that life on Earth evolves by the adaptation of species to environmental conditions. Darwin's theory relativized human importance, relegating human beings to the status of other creatures. This paradigm shift caused a shock wave that seemed to threaten the Christian understanding of the creation of humans and their special purpose in salvation. Many Christian communities in the late nineteenth and early twentieth centuries quickly responded to this theory by turning to the Bible as a counterpoint. They claimed that "true" Christians must read the Bible as a literal record of natural history and reject the findings of modern science. This approach, called fundamentalism, posited that several tenets of Christian faith must be understood as absolutely factual, including the virgin birth of Jesus, the Resurrection of Jesus, and the literal, word-for-word truth of the Bible.

Today many people are still caught in interim phases of the paradigm shift brought by the theory of evolution. Many Christians accept the theory of evolution by understanding evolution as part of God's creative process and under God's direction. For other Christians, the question of evolution remains unsettled, in part because it is a theory. The question of theory leads to the contemporary relationship between Christianity and science—the understanding of what science is.

A definition of science. A theory is a principle or postulate used to explain or interpret a phenomenon. When scientists test and retest a theory using the best tools of observation available, they arrive at evidence-based facts. Facts are considered true until proven false or called into question by new theories or new tools of observation. The process of developing a theory, testing it, confirming the tests, and theorizing anew as circumstances warrant is called the scientific method. The facts deduced by scientific method can be thought of as best-case interpretations of phenomena. Science is more properly understood as a method than a series of facts about the world, and the same method that is used to arrive at one set of facts can be used to revise those facts when new tools of observation or discoveries allow.

Science, then, is not simply about facts that people either accept or do not accept as true. Essentially, science is a way to engage the world to understand its nature and how it functions. The methods of science need not conflict with other methods of human knowing. Even if not directly employed, science can nevertheless enhance other methods that are used. In a fundamental sense, all people who study the world methodically are scientists.

Regarding the relationship between Christianity and science, Christian thought and natural science both seek to understand the world. Theology primarily concerns making sense of faith claims. The world that theology tries to understand is the same one that scientists try to understand. This commonality suggests several possible relationships between theology and science, especially as regards theories of the natural world. Three such relationship models include complementary or integrative dialogue, discreet or unrelated dialogue, and conflicting or contradictory dialogue.

Complementary or integrative dialogue. One way natural science and Christianity may engage each other is by sharing their findings in an effort to complement each other. Some people argue that theology describes the meaning and value of the world, whereas science describes the physics and structure of the world. Natural scientists ask one set of questions, and theologians ask another, but the questions concern the same world. Both sets of answers are useful in arriving at a rich understanding of the world.

Discreet or unrelated dialogue. Science and Christianity may also engage each other by claiming that each investigates something unrelated to the study of the other. Revelation is the subject matter of theology. The natural world is the subject matter of science (e.g., biology or physics), which is independent of revelation from God. In this model, science and theology need not battle each other, because their respective objects of investigation are independent of each other, as apples are of oranges.

Conflicting or contradictory dialogue. A final way that natural science and Christianity may engage each other is in conflict. When both understand themselves as studying the same phenomenon yet arrive at disparate interpretations of it, proponents on either side may conclude that science and Christianity are mutually exclusive. This can lead to an either-or approach, in which people feel forced to choose between science and religion. In recent years this has sometimes been the case in arguments concerning the theory of evolution, with biblical fundamentalists asserting a literal reading of Genesis in the Bible against the arguments of science for evolutionary theory. A more constructive approach to conflict, however, is continuing dialogue, with a willingness to revise theory or religious understanding to best accommodate all available information.

Christianity and Politics

Although some Christian communions are sectarian, or withdrawn from society at large, the relationship between many Christians and the world is more often one of active engagement and participation. Christians sometimes distinguish between being "of the world" and "in the world" to explain their sense of involvement. Although Christianity does not see itself as ultimately *of* the world (meaning generated by and destined for secular life), Christians do recognize that they are *in* the world and must live out their faith amid secular society. This dynamic invites Christians to participate in the world, even though they may not always be satisfied with its current state.

The world's challenges become opportunities for living faith in concrete, practical ways. Several of the most important ways Christians may live their faith in the polis today include evangelization and mission, participation in politics and leadership, education, and wise use of communication and media.

Evangelization and Mission

Christianity is a missionizing religion. The word *mission* means "to send" and derives from the idea that God sends people into the world to do God's work and spread God's word. Christianity uses the term *evangelization* to describe its mission work. The impulse to evangelize the world—to bring God's good message—involves cautionary considerations concerning how Christians spread their message and their reasons for doing so.

Should Christians try to convert people to their faith? If yes, why? How should they go about it? Should Christians bring social services, such as health care and legal representation, to people they evangelize or should they merely bring their faith? If they bring services, are they bribing or manipulating people into accepting Christianity? How should Christians deal with people who do not wish to convert or who regard missionizing efforts as hostile or aggressive? Should Christians missionize their coworkers or clients? How should Christians do their work in dangerous or war-torn parts of the world? All these questions arise as Christians missionize their faith.

Participation in Politics and Leadership

All people bring their values, morals, and faith with them into society. As citizens who vote, make decisions, hold jobs, serve, and lead, Christians help shape the communities in which they live. Often, specific pieces of legislation will evoke an intense response from the voting public because they touch on deeply held morals and values. Propositions concerning the legalization of drugs, definition of marriage, or penalties for hate crimes are examples of legislation that reflect the moral values of the culture.

When Christian voters come to the polls, their sense of faith and morals often guides them. Their voting is the legal expression of their civic obligation to shape their communities according to their values. In addition, when Christian citizens run for office, they often do so on platforms guided by their deepest convictions about what is best for the flourishing of individuals and society. Such candidates for political office often speak of a "Christian" platform or "Christian" values. Like candidates of every stripe, they seek to bring their vision of good society to the polis.

Education

The education of young people is critical to any society. One way Christians may engage the larger community is by becoming involved in the education curriculum offered in public schools. As taxpayers who support school districts, Christians sometimes raise their voices in support of or in opposition to certain aspects of a curriculum. The teaching of both the theory of evolution and sex education in schools, for example, has generated significant public debate in recent decades. Somewhat more recently, the teaching of the history of the American gay rights movement has prompted debate. Other education-related issues include educational vouchers and school choice, including whether taxpayer dollars ought to supplement the cost of private education, including Christian education. Some argue that Christian history and religious education in general are precluded from school curricula, even when taught from a sociological (rather than confessional) point of view. All these issues raise policy questions about the intersection between education and Christian religion.

Wise use of communication and media. Christians participate in and use modern media to engage the world. Christian uses of media as conveyors of faith-based content span the range of TV and radio broadcasting, the Internet and social networking, and Christian publishing in all forms. Modern forms of media facilitate marketing, community-building, and outreach efforts for all manner of companies and organizations. However, many Christians ask a variety of questions about media presence and usage, such as: Can liturgical celebrations be held online? How should pastors and ministers use media in their pastoral efforts? How can Christian content be responsibly and effectively communicated through media channels?

Justice and Ethics

From the time of the biblical prophets until the present, Christianity has been concerned with social justice. The prophets of the Old Testament were not soothsayers peering into their crystal balls to predict the future. Rather, they were the counterparts to Israel's leaders, and they called the political class to be accountable to God's law. The prophets expressed concern with such mundane or worldly things as fixed scales in the market place, the handling of debt, fair transmission of inheritance, property rights and land ownership, and the treatment of orphans and widows. Though the prophets spoke or wrote in many different contexts, they all agreed on one point: God does not care for shows of piety and worship when people act unjustly toward one another. Expressions of fairness and justice in the ordinary activities of life are more important to God than religious rituals and feast celebrations.

In the New Testament, Jesus distilled the law of God down to two rules: love God and love neighbor. God cannot be loved apart from one's neighbor, and by loving one's neighbor, one shows love for God. Moreover, this principle did not mean that Christians were merely to have kind or pleasant feelings toward everyone. Christians were required to actively meet the needs of other human beings, beginning with the basic needs for food and clothing. This form of active Christian charity was established in the Bible and underlies

Christians' attitude toward charity today. Part of Christian evangelism involves meeting the basic needs of people all over the world. Diverse Christian groups are worldwide expressions of Christian charity in action as people try to live Jesus' invitation to love God and neighbor.

Although there are many aspects of charity and justice that the Bible could not possibly comment on directly, the biblical model and the example of Jesus set the precedent for how and why Christians should think about social justice. One dimension of Christian thought is dedicated to moral theology, or theology about Christians' moral obligations vis-à-vis their engagement with ethical questions in the world. Dilemmas often emerge as Christians strive to live justly and meet the needs of their "neighbors." Some key areas where this occurs include health care and medical technology, family legislation and social outreach, dialogue against discrimination, criminal justice, peace and conflict resolution, and environmental issues.

Health Care and Medical Technology

Health care is a key area for Christian moral theology. On the one hand, Christians are typically concerned with people's fair access to health care, especially on behalf of poorer people for whom health care is often difficult to obtain. On the other hand, most Christians are critically aware that medical technologies invariably raise ethical questions. Should technologies be used to alter a fetus in utero or terminate a pregnancy when the developing baby has a known congenital defect? Should technologies be employed to prolong life when an individual is in a permanently vegetative condition? For how long? Who should decide when enough is enough? Who should pay? Should technologies be used or invented to clone humans, to grow or harvest organs, to produce pregnancies, or to alter or select the characteristics of a baby? Should medical technologies be used to hasten death for persons near death who are suffering from terminal illness or severe pain? One could imagine countless health care and medical issues where justice and charity for one's neighbor are called into question. Christians frequently stand at the forefront of the debate on such issues.

Family Legislation and Social Outreach

Family life is a core concern of Christian ethics, for families are the first place children encounter Christian faith and morals. Christians frequently provide charity for families, and especially children, in need. Christians recognize that family life needs the protection and support of society at large and often undertake service work to protect vulnerable persons and families, single-parent families, families dealing with long-term illness, and families with elder care responsibilities. Some Christians also actively engage legislators about laws that affect family life, including laws regarding marriage, abortion, adoption, custody of children, divorce, child support, inheritance rights, and health insurance coverage.

GAY MARRIAGE?

A recent example of the heated dialogue on family issues that intersects with Christian religious values is legislation concerning the definition of marriage in the United States. In some states, for example, New York, Massachusetts, Connecticut, Iowa, and Vermont, same-sex marriages are legally recognized. In California, gay marriage was temporarily possible, but presently same-sex marriage licenses are denied. Conversely, other states, for example, Ohio, have taken steps to define marriage as between one man and one woman. The U.S. government passed a federal law in 1996, known as the Defense of Marriage Act, which defines marriage as a legal union between one man and one woman (although at the time of this writing Congress is considering a bill to repeal this legislation). Beyond the United States, ten countries worldwide recognize same-sex marriage, while in dozens of others, homosexual activity is still considered a crime. In at least seven countries, homosexual acts are punishable by death.

Christians of all persuasions have weighed in on this issue. Many Christians feel that marriage is designed by God to be

Continued

Continued

between one man and one woman, intended by God for the pro-creation of children. Christians of this mindset turn to the Bible to support their argument in favor of the traditional male-female model of marriage (including the Creation stories in Genesis, the prohibitions against homosexuality in the book of Leviticus and elsewhere, and teachings on marriage scattered throughout the Old and New Testaments). The arguments in favor of traditional marriage are typically endorsed by the church leaders of major denominations, who rely on the millennia-long history in the West of heterosexual marriage. Other Christians argue in favor of the possibility of same-sex marriage. These Christians will make the case variously that biblical passages on marriage and sexuality are not conclusive or unambiguous, that many aspects of the Bible do not speak to contemporary culture with authority, and that there are many biblical teachings that modern people reject as binding (for example, killing children as a penalty for disobedience as prescribed in Deuteronomy 21:18–21). Christians who argue for same-sex marriage may support their stance on the basis of the dignity, rights, and justice concerns for homosexual persons.

Contemporary Christian debate on same-sex marriage ranges from such terse assertions as "the Bible is against it" to sublime arguments that attempt to synthesize the theological tradition with the best modern understandings of gender, biology, brain chemistry, psychology, sociology, and even jurisprudence. Moreover, Christians are aware that even if their religion could conclusively settle all questions about marriage for Christians, there are many non-Christians in society, as well. Christians are but one subpopulation, raising the questions, Should Christian morality be legally required of non-Christians? and, How much are Christian perspectives in concert with other demographic perspectives? This ongoing contemporary discussion is an important example that reveals the depth, range, and even tension that can exist internally among Christians, as well as between Christians and the polis at large.

Dialogue against Discrimination

In the past century, antidiscrimination movements have profoundly influenced Christian thought. Minority populations and women increasingly have been able to articulate the social injustices they have historically suffered; in response, many Christians have become active in promoting the fair and equal treatment of all persons regardless of race or gender. The idea that members of the community become "one" in baptism, which dates back to the first years of Christianity, set the precedent for egalitarianism within the Christian churches. Unfortunately, Christians throughout the eras have fallen prey to the same tendencies of gender and racial discrimination that are manifested in society at large. Today, however, many Christian communities recognize past error in this regard and work for the full social enfranchisement of all people, despite ethnic, gender, and lifestyle differences. Many such communities today also strive to identify and to end discrimination against homosexual persons within their churches.

Criminal Justice

Christians have a historical interest in the treatment of prisoners and persons accused of crime that stems from the biblical concern for vulnerable persons. In the Gospel accounts, Jesus expressed concern for the treatment of prisoners, and Jesus himself was found guilty of criminal acts and sentenced to death. Christians recognize that it is easy to love people who do well by one but not easy to love one's enemy. The invitation to love one's neighbor is an invitation to love even "unlovable" individuals. The rationale for such love stems from the belief that God created all persons, and so all persons bear an inherent dignity. Even if people disfigure the image of God within themselves, human beings must honor one another's value as creatures of God.

God's biblical covenant was enduring and steadfast, despite Israel's regular failure to do what was right. What is more, God offers opportunities for reconciliation in the face of moral failure. Christians see Jesus' death on the cross as the ultimate opportunity for reconciliation, to which all people are invited. Thus Christians often extend themselves generously to people in prison and lobby for prisoners' humane treatment as persons of value and for whom reconciliation and forgiveness are possible. Many Christians reject the death penalty on these same grounds.

Peace and Conflict Resolution

Christians are concerned about the welfare of the world and often actively work toward peace and conflict resolution. The first Christian communities lacked the ability, resources, and motivation to wage war. Furthermore, they modeled their response to violence on Jesus, who willingly gave himself over to the authorities even though he faced an unjust death. Jesus' life and death established a precedent of pacifism in Christian thought, as well as a special appreciation of martyrdom for one's faith.

Since at least the time of Constantine in the fourth century, however, Christians have participated in war. Seldom have Christians waged war as Christians. But as part of larger political bodies, Christians have joined in war, sometimes fighting against other Christians. Examples here include the Crusades of the Middle Ages, in which Western Christians fought Eastern Christians; the religious wars in Europe among different Christian factions in the sixteenth and seventeenth centuries; and the Catholic-Protestant conflict in Northern Ireland in the twentieth century. As citizens of the political states in which they live, moreover, Christians are often members of the military, although sometimes serving in noncombatant capacities. Occasionally, pacifist Christian communities, like the Amish, refuse military service altogether. Participation in combat has led some Christians to ask what the morally licit grounds are, if any, for taking up arms against others. This just war theorizing has played a large role in Christian attitudes toward violence. Many Christians find no allowable grounds for violence; still others pursue peace-building strategies and conflict resolution initiatives. Inspired by the knowledge that there can be no lasting peace without justice, many Christians today actively participate in efforts to end conflict through the establishment of broad social justice initiatives.

Environmental Issues

Christian interest in environmental issues has burgeoned in recent decades. There is long precedent in the Hebraic and biblical traditions for ecological awareness and environmental care, rooted in the belief that God created the world and according to the Bible, "It was good" (Genesis 1:12). The Bible commands human beings to be stewards of God's creation, and this stewardship extends toward care of other people, animals, and the land. People in industrialized nations have become increasingly aware of the environmental costs of water, land, and air pollution, soil erosion, industrial agriculture, endangerment of animal species, human population problems, and military action. Christian theologians and activists have begun to articulate theological responses to these issues, suggesting that abuse of the environment is a moral evil that requires repudiation and correction on the part of Christians at the societal and individual levels.

Conclusion

Christian dialogue with the world will always be in process, just as the issues to which Christians will need to respond will always be in flux. This is so because Christians of every era are, foremost, people of their times. Their cultures, social backdrops, technologies, economies, and so on provide the context in which they encounter and live their religious belief.

Although basic elements of the religious tradition are handed down in a stable and careful transmission, the context in which that tradition is received always changes. A couple decades ago, it would not have made sense to ask whether a liturgical service could be held online, but today that question is relevant. Just decades ago, it would have been inconceivable to ask whether stem cell research was morally licit, because stem cell research had not yet been invented. The lived context will always bring new questions for people living their faith. The Christian person will always face the task of relating contemporary questions to the historical tradition. People with an active and reflective faith will thus be challenged continually to play the role of translator-theologian as they seek to know and do right ever anew.

The Bible and the entire theological tradition that accompanies it encourage a basic belief in the dignity of the individual and the need for a good society, understood analogically as "love of neighbor." When love of neighbor is coupled with love of God, Christians have a powerful set of guidelines for understanding their faith and putting it into meaningful practice in every aspect of life.

Questions for Discussion and Review

1. Why is religion inevitably concerned with the world?
2. Describe the reasons behind the tension between science and Christian faith today.
3. Can a poem or a song be "true"? If yes, in what way? Does something have to be historically verifiable for it to be true?
4. Compare and contrast three different models for a Christianity–science dialogue.
5. Describe three ways some Christians engage in the political arena. Can you think of others, not stated in this text?
6. Do you think Christian taxpayers should help shape the curriculum of the public schools their children attend?
7. What are the benefits, losses, and general tensions of bringing one's religious sensibility to legislation?
8. Describe some aspects of social justice that engage Christians.
9. What are the biggest concerns, in your opinion, that Christians face in the world today? How do you think Christians should address those concerns?
10. How does love of God relate to love of neighbor in the Christian faith?

Key Terms

Charles Darwin

complementary
dialogue

contradictory
dialogue

evangelize

mission

morality

*On the Origin of
Species*

paradigm shift

scientific method

Resources

Deane-Drummond, Celia. *Eco-Theology*. Winona, MN: Saint Mary's Press, 2008.

Forster, Greg. *The Contested Square: The Crisis of Christianity and Politics*. Downers Grove, IL: InterVarsity Press, 2008.

Glanzer, Perry L., and Todd C. Ream. *Christianity and Moral Identity in Higher Education*. New York: Palgrave Macmillan, 2009.

Hunt, Mary E., and Diann L. Neu. *New Feminist Christianity: Many Voices, Many Views*. Woodstock, VT: Skylight Paths, 2010.

McGrath, Alister. *Science and Religion: A New Introduction*. 2nd ed. Oxford, UK: Wiley-Blackwell, 2010.

Panicola, Michael R., et al. *Health Care Ethics: Theological Foundations, Contemporary Issues, and Controversial Cases*. Winona, MN: Anselm Academic, 2007, 2011.

Index

An m, n or t following a page number indicates a map, footnote or table, respectively.

Z